THE SAVINGS AND LOAN BUSINESS

Leon T. Kendall
for the
United States Savings and Loan League

THE SAVINGS AND LOAN BUSINESS
ITS PURPOSES, FUNCTIONS,
AND ECONOMIC JUSTIFICATION

A MONOGRAPH
PREPARED FOR THE

Commission on Money and Credit

GREENWOOD PRESS, PUBLISHERS
WESTPORT, CONNECTICUT

Library of Congress Cataloging in Publication Data

Kendall, Leon T
   The savings and loan business.

   "Prepared for the Commission on Money and Credit."
   Reprint of the ed. published by Prentice-Hall,
Englewood Cliffs, N. J., in series: Trade associations
monographs.
   1. Building and loan associations--United States.
I. United States Savings and Loan League. II. Com-
mission on Money and Credit. III. Title. IV. Series:
Trade associations monographs.
[HG2151.K4 1977]   332.3'2'0973   77-14207
ISBN 0-8371-9843-7

Reprinted with the permission of Prentice-Hall, Inc.

Reprinted in 1977 by   Greenwood Press, Inc.
                      51 Riverside Avenue
                      Westport, CT. 06880

Printed in the United States of America

FOREWORD

One facet of the Commission on Money and Credit's investigation was an inquiry into the functioning of our financial system in order to arrive at a judgment of the adequacy of that system and its regulation to serve the needs of a growing economy.

In addition to examining other sources of information and having special studies prepared, the Commission also sought the advice, experience, and opinion of practitioners in the financial area. In this latter connection the United States Savings and Loan League was invited to prepare a monograph on the savings and loan industry.

In soliciting the monograph, the Commission indicated the desirability of having it provide information on the following six topics:

1. The nature of government regulation of savings and loan associations, including tax treatment, and its impact upon the functioning of the industry.
2. The operations and practices of the industry, in terms of flow of funds, portfolio practices, liquidity requirements, and so forth.
3. The role of savings and loan associations in the economy, in terms of their influence upon economic growth, their contribution to economic stability, and their impact upon the allocation of resources.
4. The effects of monetary-debt management policy upon the industry and the role of savings and loan associations in transmitting these policies throughout the economy.
5. The structure and competitive position of savings and loan associations, both within the industry and vis-à-vis other financial intermediaries.
6. The view of the savings and loan industry regarding possible changes in regulatory or tax provisions.

The United States Savings and Loan League responded willingly to the invitation of the Commission and was most cooperative in working out with the staff of the Commission the scope and detailed outline of the planned monograph. The preparation of the monograph itself was a large task, and the finished product was a valuable contribution to the Commission.

In making its request to the USSLL for a monograph on the savings and loan industry, the Commission indicated its desire and expectation to publish important background and research materials which it used in the course of its work. We are pleased that the League consented to the inclusion of the monograph among the supporting documents of the Commission and agreed to revise for publication the original paper in order to make this further contribution to the general fund of knowledge on the nature of the savings and loan industry and its role in the economy.

On behalf of the Commission and its staff we would like to express our thanks to the United States Savings and Loan League for the preparation of this study.

BERTRAND FOX
Research Director

ELI SHAPIRO
Deputy Research Director

December 1961

PREFACE

The savings and loan business welcomes continued investigation by sincere researchers and scholars into its role in the American financial community. Although the contents of this monograph represent a reasoned analysis of our purposes and functions in light of today's knowledge, we realize full well that the future will bring further refinement in these premises and more appropriate interpretation and explanation of our role in the light of greater knowledge.

A note on terminology is appropriate. In this monograph, savings and loan associations will be referred to from time to time simply as savings associations. The phrase "savings account" will be in common usage, but the term "share account" will be conspicuous by its absence.

I am indebted to many people, both within and without the savings and loan business, for their cooperation and assistance in the preparation of this monograph. Particular acknowledgments are due Professor Frank H. Gane of Northwestern University; Carl F. Distelhorst, Executive Vice President, Florida Savings and Loan League; and Norman Strunk, Executive Vice President, United States Savings and Loan League, and members of his staff for their willingness in reviewing this manuscript as it evolved.

Parts of the monograph were prepared originally by Jean Gillis Harth ("Legal Organization"), Jeanne Griest (the section on secular, cyclical, and seasonal influences on liquidity and Appendix B on "Adjustment for Seasonal Variation—Methodology"), and James Hollensteiner and Lee Duss ("The Depression Experience"). The author, however, assumes full responsibility for the present state of the work. To Bernice Barnes and Dorothy Logan goes a special vote of thanks for their editing and data-assembling efforts.

Finally, it is with the sincerest of feelings that we dedicate this monograph to the memory of the late Fred T. Greene, former President of the Federal Home Loan Bank of Indianapolis, member of the Commission on Money and Credit, and a lifetime student of finance and the savings and loan business. Mr. Greene, probably more than anyone else, was responsible for developing in the author an understanding of the role savings associations play in our economy and the philosophy under which they operate.

L. K.

CONTENTS

List of Charts

List of Tables

Chapter 1

INTRODUCTION

Purpose and Scope of the Monograph

This monograph represents an attempt to set down in a comprehensive manner the purposes, functions, and economic justification of savings and loan associations. Knowledge and understanding of the savings and loan business among outsiders, particularly those in academic circles, has not kept pace with its growth and importance to our nation. It is our hope that by drawing together the basic data describing the business, and adding to these the industry explanations and interpretation of their significance, a major step can be taken toward filling this gap.

The work was undertaken at the request of the Commission on Money and Credit so that its staff and consultants might have at their fingertips the basic data relevant to the business and a better understanding of the way it views its role in our economy. We are grateful to the Commission for giving us a formal opportunity to present to them a picture of the savings and loan business.

Basic Philosophy of the Savings and Loan Business

Why do we have savings and loan associations? The fundamental reason for their existence is to finance the purchase of existing homes and the construction of new homes with the funds accumulated. The Congress of the United States and the various state legislatures provided for the creation of savings associations so that the home ownership base of the nation might be broadened. The underlying premise of savings and loan operations, as carried out today, is that widespread, economical home ownership is the primary *raison d'être* of the business. There is reason to believe that legislation sanctioning the modern development of these associations would not have come to pass if their principal objective were to promote thrift. Once this concept is accepted, much of how

1

savings associations operate becomes more readily understood. Attempts to judge the savings and loan business by the tenets of commercial banking theory fall short, for they fail to give appropriate credit to the basic purpose of a specialized, essentially mutual, home financing institution.

Savings and loan associations differ from other deposit-type savings institutions in one very important respect. The other deposit-type institutions have as one of their primary objectives the mobilizing of funds (savings) and the providing of a return to depositors and shareholders. They are thrift institutions first, and they hold themselves to be simply that. The attitudes of such institutions toward diversification in risk assets, liquidity, borrowing from reserve pools of credit, such as the Federal Home Loan Bank System and the Federal Reserve, are a reflection of their concern for depositors and shareholders and for the safety of their investments. In contrast, savings and loan associations, as specialized institutions, hold quite different attitudes toward diversification of risk assets and borrowing from central credit pools. Although they, too, are concerned about the welfare of savers, their concern is prompted by the need to secure funds to support home financing and home ownership in this nation. Simply, if the home financing element were eliminated from savings and loan activity and the general investment market were made its province, there probably would not be so great an economic and social justification for the existence of these associations. Savers and thrift could be served readily by any of a number of other institutions.

Savings and loan associations contribute to the well-being of the country by making it possible for an ever-widening group of Americans to acquire their own homes. A market is developed for the production of the home building industry through the financing of existing properties as well as of new units.

Associations contribute to the maintenance of stable real estate values as well. The prices of houses might well be bid up to higher levels during periods of increasing demand for houses if there were not a concurrent rise in the supply of houses. New dwelling units cannot be created in volume unless there is adequate financing both for the new houses and for the existing houses that must change hands so that people can buy new ones.

Financing houses out of people's savings is noninflationary, for that portion of the personal income which is siphoned into savings associations for use in financing homes cannot at the same time be used for spending in other sectors of the economy. Without savings and loan associations, housing probably would have to be financed either by bank-created credit or directly by the government. Government financing probably would require the sale of additional securities to the bank system by the Treasury. Thus, financing houses out of credit, whether it is created directly by banks or by banks through government financing, is inflationary because it creates additional demand in the housing sector without reducing the demand in other parts of the economy.

The close tie between home building activity and the savings and loan business can be demonstrated through a regional analysis of the growth of the savings and loan business. In general, those areas where housing starts and real estate activity have been strongest are also the areas where savings and loan associations have grown the most. During the ten years from the end of 1950 to the end of 1960, savings and loan assets throughout the nation climbed from $16.9 billion to $71.5 billion, or 323 percent. Growth rates by region varied from a 20 percent annual rate of gain in the fast-growing Pacific states and 17 percent in the Southwest to 10 percent in the more settled New England states and 13 percent in the Middle Atlantic area. And by 1961, year-end total assets of the business will reach an all-time peak of $80 billion.

Problems Facing the Savings and Loan Business

Among the more important problems confronting the savings and loan business are:

1) Attracting a large enough net inflow of savings funds to meet the anticipated home financing requirements of the American people.

2) Holding the cost of home financing funds as low as is reasonably possible.

3) Increasing the mobility of home financing funds to make them available for use in communities where they are needed most. Because home building activity tends to be concentrated in the strongest economic growth areas, where existing capital resources are already strained, the mobility of funds is essential if local home financing needs are to be served economically.

Chapter 2

SAVINGS AND LOAN HISTORY

The First Hundred Years

Origin and Early Development

Savings and loan associations in the United States are direct descendants of the British building societies. The building societies were the outgrowth of "friendly societies"—small, local cooperative groups whose members made weekly contributions which entitled them and their families to benefits in the event of death, illness, accident, fire, sometimes unemployment, or certain other major calamities.

The Oxford Provident Building Association was organized in 1831 in Frankford, Pennsylvania (since 1854, a part of Philadelphia) by a group of thirty-seven local businessmen and wage earners. This savings and loan association, the first known in the United States, was patterned after the British building society and was organized very simply. Since there were no written manuals or instructions, three of the original members, who were Englishmen, supplied the knowledge necessary to start a building society. Members subscribed to shares toward which they made monthly payments. As soon as the sum of $500 was available for a loan, members submitted bids for the use of the fund to purchase a home already available or to finance the building of a new home. In February 1832, the first loan—$375—was made to buy a two and one-half story frame building with less than 500 square feet of floor space. (The building is still standing at 4276 Orchard Street, Philadelphia.)

There was no provision in the original bylaws of the Oxford Provident for the admission of new members, but later revisions allowed a member to sell his share provided the old members approved the prospective buyer as a credit risk. Approval by the old members was important, since every share subscriber was entitled to a loan. Careful appraisals were made before loans were granted, and before the end of its first year of operation the association was requiring insurance on the property of

4

borrowers. In contrast to the early British societies which made loans only to build homes, Oxford Provident loans were as readily available to buy homes already built.

A delegation went to Frankford in 1836, secured the information necessary and, that same year, founded in Brooklyn the second known association, the Brooklyn Building and Mutual Loan Association. The third was organized in South Carolina in 1843. From then on, growth was widespread. When the Civil War began there were associations in several states, and by the 1880's probably in every state. The early associations were all voluntary and unincorporated. There was no public supervision of their activities. When the last member paid his loan and the shares matured, the organization quietly went out of business, often leaving no trace of its existence.

During the 1850's, associations organized on a serial plan started to become popular. In contrast to the terminating associations which issued a single series of stock and dissolved when each member had received a loan, the serial plan involved issuing successive series of stock so that the association continued in existence despite the termination of individual series.

The next stage of development resulted from a growing preference of members for the permanent share plan. This plan, which began its rise to prominence in the 1870's, eliminated the series subscription to stock in favor of the issuance of shares at any time. Shareholders' accounts were kept separately and earnings were credited separately.

In some regions the permanent or guarantee capital stock plan became popular. These associations, originating in 1890, issued a nonwithdrawable class of stock subscribed to by the founders, with definite contractual liabilities to the other types of association members.

The savings and loan business from time to time seems to have had fringe elements trading on its goodwill. One of the most ambitious of such groups was the "nationals." Appearing on the scene in the mid-1880's, their philosophy had very little in common with that of savings and loan cooperatives, even though they traded on the good name of established locals. The great majority of nationals were speculative schemes designed to benefit their promoters. At their peak, they numbered almost 250, taking in money from all over the country and making loans across the nation. Nearly all were liquidated in the depression of 1893-97, victims of a depressed real estate market as well as of their own immoderate expenses, questionable loans, and widely scattered and poorly controlled operations.

Government Supervision

New York was the first state to recognize the growing importance of savings and loan associations by enacting specific regulatory measures.

In 1875, annual reports of condition were required; and in 1892, supervision and annual inspection by the Superintendent of Banks became compulsory. More than half the states had passed some savings and loan supervisory law by 1900; all but two had provided for some degree of regulation by 1931.

Growth of the Business

There is little reliable data available about the scope of the savings and loan business during the first half-century of its existence. The earliest statistical study, made in 1888, estimated the existence of 3,000 to 3,500 associations, with assets of $300 million, a rather impressive figure for that period. The first comprehensive study of the business, made in 1893 by the U.S. Commissioner of Labor, indicated about 5,600 associations operating in all the states, with a membership of approximately 1,350,000 and assets of about $475 million. The nationals were not considered true savings and loans, and were therefore excluded from the study.

Savings and loans, along with other financial institutions, lost ground after the panic of 1893. Beginning in 1904, however, they gained steadily (rapidly in the 1920's) until the Great Depression of the 1930's. Association mortgage loans amounted to only $125 million in 1901, but reached $1 billion in 1923 and crossed the $2 billion mark in 1927.

The United States League

The United States Savings and Loan League (originally the United States League of Local Building and Loan Associations) has been a vital factor in the development of the business. It was organized in Chicago in 1892 by representatives of thirteen state leagues. Although the establishment of a strong national trade association was inevitable, the formation of the League was probably hastened by the need for taking action against the adverse efforts of the nationals and the need for a means to the enactment of legislation.

The Modern Era

Depression Experience

Savings and loans began to feel the effects of the depression in late 1930 and early 1931. Withdrawals began to rise, reaching a high point in 1933 and roughly maintaining this peak through 1934. Despite the relatively long terms of loans at savings and loan associations, loan repayments slowed down and more and more loans became delinquent; in many cases, foreclosure was the only recourse. Banks' failures compounded association difficulties. Between 1930 and 1933, more than 8,800 commercial banks failed, taking with them the deposit funds of savings associations and association customers. Mortgage payments could not be made and refinancing became exceedingly difficult.

Foreclosures on all the nation's urban homes soared from a pre-depression average of 75,000 a year to 273,000 in 1932 and 271,000 in 1933. The yearly average from 1931 to 1935 was 231,000.

Having acquired large amounts of property on which borrowers were unable to meet payments, savings and loans found themselves deep in the real estate business. Normally a nominal figure, real estate owned by associations rose above $1 billion for four consecutive years, 1934 through 1937; and in 1936 it represented more than 20 percent of total association assets. Associations "froze." Although solvent, they were unable to liquidate real estate assets as rapidly as savers wanted funds.

Although real estate values declined sharply, savings and loans did not generally take substantial losses. They held the properties and maintained them, realized a fair rental income, and finally marketed them at approximately their cost.

Savings and loan assets declined from a predepression peak of nearly $9 billion in 1930 to under $6 billion in 1935. Resources of the average association declined from $750,000 to $560,000. Not until 1938 was this downward trend reversed. The depression experience of associations is considered in greater detail in Chapter 9.

Federal agencies played an important role in association activities during the 1930's. The Reconstruction Finance Corporation began making funds available to associations in 1932, six months prior to establishment of the Federal Home Loan Bank System. Total savings and loan borrowings from the RFC amounted to $118 million; all but $2 million was repaid by 1937.

The Federal Home Loan Bank System was established in 1932. The Home Owners Loan Corporation was instituted in 1933. During its active lending life (1933 through 1936), it refinanced three-quarters of a billion dollars of home mortgages—on more than a million homes—formerly held by private lenders. The Corporation actually advanced almost $3.1 billion, including reconditioning loans, taxes, assessments, and closing costs and HOLC purchases of savings and loan mortgages totaled around $770 million. Federal savings and loan associations were authorized as part of the Home Owners Loan Act of 1933. The Federal Savings and Loan Insurance Corporation was established in 1934, about a year after the Federal Deposit Insurance Corporation.

Between 1933 and 1937, nearly $275 million in federal funds was invested in savings and loan accounts at 1,400 associations. The program took two phases: (1) the United States Treasury invested $49.3 million in federal associations; (2) the HOLC was authorized to invest up to

$300 million in federal- and state-chartered associations which either were insured or were FHLB members. The funds were aimed at new institutions.

By the late 1930's the real estate market improved and, prior to the entry of the United States into World War II, savings and loan associations experienced a taste of prosperity. Real estate holdings were reduced substantially; loan volume regained strength; construction lending was given new emphasis. The modernization of savings and loan operations, inspired by the depression, became more general. Attitudes changed toward liquidity, reserves, interest and dividend rates, lending and savings plans, advertising, and the role of managers and directors.

Wartime Experience

Shortages of building materials and priority systems stopped most private home building following Pearl Harbor. Competition for loans on existing properties became intense. Declining interest rates, the surplus of investible funds, and learning to live with controls were the principal problems facing association managers. Military and defense activities produced personnel shortages and, in many instances, women kept the business going. Associations earned Treasury citations for selling to the public $1.6 billion in war bonds. They also bought $3.25 billion worth of government bonds for their own portfolios, lifting the ratio of government securities to mortgage holdings to a high of 43.8 percent in 1945. Between 1941 and 1945, associations repaid to the United States Treasury more than $180 million of the federal funds received from that agency during the mid-1930's.

The savings and loan business was the first to make an intensive study of the GI home loan program (enacted in 1944), contributing valuable information both to the legislative draft and to the working regulations. Associations were the first institutions to make GI loans in large volume. During 1946, the first year of substantial volume, they were responsible for $1.25 billion of the over-all total of $2.3 billion of GI loans made.

Postwar Growth

The expansion of the savings and loan business was an outstanding feature of the postwar decade. Associations did their share to meet the challenge of the great housing shortage and the revived demand for mortgage funds. Because they came out of the war with ample liquid resources (over $2 billion), they were able to undertake quickly large-scale financing of home mortgages. In addition, savings and loan management had developed a broader outlook on their mission, and began placing greater emphasis on attractive quarters, choice locations, and business promotion activities. Effective trade organizations existed at the national and state levels.

Key statutory changes took place in 1950, many of which had been sought for years. These included the reduction of the FSLIC insurance premium, raising of FSLIC insurance coverage to $10,000, revision of FSLIC repayment terms to eliminate competitive disadvantage with banks, Treasury backstops for the FHLB System and the FSLIC, and provision for paying back all government investment in the two agencies to make them wholly member-owned. In 1955, the Federal Home Loan Bank Board was restored to its previous status as an independent government agency, fulfilling another long-standing savings and loan goal.

Comparable improvements were taking place on the state level. During the 1950's state laws were simplified in terminology, more complete provisions for supervision were enacted, more flexible mortgage contracts and savings plans were authorized, and investment powers were expanded in the real estate lending field. Thus, underlying growth

TABLE 2-1
Number and Total Assets of Savings and Loan Associations
1900-1960

Year	Number of Associations	Insured by FSLIC Federal Charter	State Charter	Noninsured State[1]	Total Assets (Millions of Dollars)
1900	5,356			5,356	$ 571
1905	5,264			5,264	629
1910	5,869			5,869	932
1915	6,806			6,806	1,484
1920	8,633			8,633	2,520
1925	12,403			12,403	5,509
1930	11,777			11,777	8,829
1935	10,266	987	130	9,149	5,875
1940	7,521	1,437	840	5,244	5,733
1945	- 6,149	1,467	1,008	3,674	8,747
1946	6,093	1,471	1,025	3,597	10,202
1947	- 6,045	1,478	1,058	3,509	11,687
1948	6,011	1,485	1,131	3,395	13,028
1949	5,983	1,508	1,248	3,227	14,622
1950	5,992	1,526	1,334	3,132	16,893
1951	5,995	1,549	1,471	2,975	19,222
1952	6,004	1,581	1,591	2,832	22,660
1953	6,012	1,604	1,700	2,708	26,733
1954	6,038	1,640	1,793	2,605	31,736
1955	6,071	1,683	1,871	2,517	37,719
1956	6,136	1,739	1,927	2,470	42,875
1957	6,169	1,772	2,000	2,397	48,138
1958	6,208	1,807	2,074	2,327	55,115
1959	6,224	1,841	2,138	2,245	63,472
1960	6,276	1,873	2,225	2,178	71,489

[1]Includes Massachusetts Co-operative Banks insured by the Co-operative Central Bank. In 1958, there were 175 Massachusetts institutions.
In 1959, 61 billion, or 96 percent, of total assets were insured by the FSLIC and other governmental agencies.

Sources: Federal Home Loan Bank Board; Co-operative Central Bank of Massachusetts.

was the sound, basic purpose of savings and loan associations—the promotion of thrift and home ownership.

Present Structure

There were over 6,200 savings and loan associations in the United States at the close of 1960, the number having increased every year since 1949 (Table 2-1). Associations are to be found in every state of the Union, the District of Columbia, and Puerto Rico. Pennsylvania, with 844 institutions, has the greatest number of associations; Illinois, with 588, has the second largest number.

A savings and loan association may be defined as a locally owned and privately managed thrift and home financing institution. Most of them are mutual institutions, that is, owned by the savers. As such, they accept savings accounts from individuals and other sources, and invest these funds principally in monthly-payment, amortized loans for the construction, purchase, or repair and modernization of homes. Savings and loan associations lead the nation in providing funds for home financing purposes and are important in the promotion of savings.

A dual system of savings and loan associations exists from the point of view of their legal charters. Approximately 4,400 institutions (70 percent) operate under state charters and 1,800 operate under federal charters. In the case of state-chartered institutions, supervision is vested in a department of the respective state governments; in the case of federal institutions, the agency exercising supervisory authority is the Federal Home Loan Bank Board in Washington. Supervision involves, as a minimum, annual examination and audit, and the continuous assurance that provisions of both charter and law are being observed. On the basis of assets, federals represent approximately 55 percent of total savings and loan resources; state-chartered institutions represent the remaining 45 percent.

The average size of savings and loan associations tends to vary with their legal structure. Federally chartered institutions are the largest, with average assets in excess of $18 million. The typical state-chartered, non-federally regulated institution is the smallest, with average assets only slightly over $1 million. Federally chartered associations have been growing most rapidly, while the noninsured institutions have experienced relatively little growth. The reasons why institutions do not have federal insurance vary. At times, the specific policies of the Federal Savings and Loan Insurance Corporation regarding operating procedures conflict with those at individual institutions. Some associations are open only one or two evenings a week, some accept savings in specialized ways from individuals, and some have atypical lending operations. Such institutions would not qualify for insurance under today's rules.

Assets of the 4100 associations whose accounts are currently insured by the Federal Savings and Loan Insurance Corporation comprise over 95 percent of the total assets of the business. All federal associations, as well as state-chartered, insured institutions holding 89 percent of state-chartered assets, had FSLIC insurance on their accounts. Including the assets of the 175 cooperative banks (state-chartered, mutual thrift and home financing institutions) in Massachusetts, which are insured by the Co-operative Central Bank of Massachusetts, an agency of that state, over 96 percent of the total assets fall into the insured category. The 26 percent of all associations which are outside the federal sphere hold less than 4 percent of the total assets of the business.

Since most savings associations are mutual organizations, approximately 87 percent of the total assets of the business were held by such institutions at the end of 1959. On that date there were 466 insured capital stock associations with assets of slightly over $8 billion. While capital stock associations are authorized in eighteen states, three states (California, Ohio, and Texas) contain over 90 percent of the capital stock association assets.

Many stock companies date back to pre-depression days and the turn of the century, but such institutions received little public attention until 1955. In that year the first savings and loan holding companies were formed through the purchase of capital stock savings and loan associations. The holding company movement began in California and continues to be concentrated in that state. Such financial arrangements permitted widespread public ownership of stock savings and loan companies. At the present time approximately twenty savings and loan holding companies controlling approximately sixty-five associations offer their securities for public sale on organized stock exchanges and over-the-counter markets. The passage of the Holding Company Act in 1959, limiting the holding company to ownership of one savings and loan association and no more than 10 percent of any others, has slowed the development of this form of financial arrangement.

Association Size. Savings associations vary in size. The bulk of the assets are represented by well-located institutions in attractive offices. Usually they are to be found in financial districts or in busy shopping centers of urban communities. A typical association has approximately $10 million in assets, serves several thousand savers and investors as customers, and holds mortgage loans on approximately 1,500 homes within a fifty-mile radius of its office.

Savings and loan branch offices are becoming more numerous. Of the 6,276 savings associations, 800 institutions have branches in the thirty-seven states (as well as in the District of Columbia and Puerto Rico) where multiple offices are permitted. Branches are most numerous in California; Ohio has the second largest number. At the close of 1951, there were 251 branch offices; today there are over 1,300 savings and loan branches in operation.

During the past decade the average size of savings and loan associations has grown consistently. In 1950, the average association held $2.8 million in assets; ten years later it had assets of $11.4 million. Of even greater interest than the size of the average association is the analysis of savings and loan assets by size of association (Table 2-2). In 1960, 3,248 associations (51.8 percent) were under $5 million in asset size but accounted for only 8.9 percent of total assets. At the other end of the scale, only 250 associations (4 percent) had over $50 million in assets, but these institutions accounted for 38 percent of total assets. These findings are based upon figures for members of the Federal Home Loan Bank System.

Growth in the savings and loan business has come from the increased size of established associations rather than from an increase in the number of institutions in existence. In 1946, 48 percent of the assets of the business were in associations under $5 million in asset size; by 1959, only 8.9 percent were in such institutions. The average association has grown six-fold since the end of World War II, while there have been less than 200 new institutions established.

Concentration of Assets.   Despite the growth in assets at larger savings and loan associations, the concentration of assets in the business continues to be much less than it is in the commercial banking business or among mutual savings banks. Table 2-3 permits a comparison of the degree of concentration of assets at commercial banks, mutual savings banks, and savings and loan associations. In the case of commercial banks, total deposits rather than assets were used in these comparisons since the latter were not readily available. Assets are not compiled on this basis.

On December 31, 1959, there were 12,998 insured commercial banks operating in the United States, with total assets of $243 billion. The average bank was rather small with assets of around $19 million. In commercial banking, the degree of concentration can be measured by noting the number of banks and the proportion of deposits held by institutions of over $100 million in deposit size. In 1959, 267 banks, 2.1 percent of all banks, reported deposits of $100 million or more and held 59 percent of the total deposits of the banking system. Banks with over $50 million in deposits, 484 in number and 3.1 percent of all banks, held 66 percent of total deposits. The remaining 12,514 banks (96.2 percent of all banks), could count as their share only 34 percent of total deposits.

At mutual savings banks, the concentration of assets was even more pronounced. Institutions with assets in excess of $100 million totaled

TABLE 2-2
Distribution of Savings and Loan Assets
By Size of Association

December 31, 1960

Asset Size of Association	Number of Associations	Assets (Millions of Dollars)	Percent		Cumulative Percent	
			Associations	Assets	Associations	Assets
$100,000,000 and over	88	$16,400	1.4%	22.9%	1.4%	22.9%
50,000,000 - 100,000,000	162	11,061	2.6	15.5	4.0	38.4
25,000,000 - 50,000,000	416	13,025	6.6	18.2	10.6	56.6
10,000,000 - 25,000,000	1,145	16,875	18.2	23.6	28.8	80.2
5,000,000 - 10,000,000	1,217	7,775	19.4	10.9	48.2	91.1
1,000,000 - 5,000,000	2,332	5,900	37.2	8.3	85.4	99.4
Less than 1,000,000	916	450	14.6	0.6	100.0%	100.0%
Total	6,276	$71,489	100.0%	100.0%		

Source: Federal Home Loan Bank Board.

TABLE 2-3
Percentage Distribution of Assets of Selected Financial Institutions
By Asset Size
December 31, 1959

Asset Size[1]	Commercial Banks				Mutual Savings Banks[2]				Savings and Loan Associations			
	Number	Per-cent	Assets (Thousands)	Per-cent	Number	Per-cent	Assets (Thousands)	Per-cent	Number	Per-cent	Assets (Thousands)	Per-cent
$100,000,000 and over	267	2.1%	$142,588,947	58.8%	88	16.9%	$27,527,236	71.2%	71	1.5%	$12,961,821	21.1%
50,000,000 - 100,000,000	217	1.7	16,955,502	7.0	59	11.3	4,238,160	11.0	156	3.4	10,409,534	16.9
25,000,000 - 50,000,000	496	3.8	18,783,736	7.7	106	20.4	3,712,367	9.6	351	7.6	11,942,636	19.4
10,000,000 - 25,000,000	1,534	11.8	25,256,226	10.5	157	30.3	2,527,634	6.5	950	20.7	14,783,465	24.0
5,000,000 - 10,000,000	2,394	18.4	18,293,400	7.5	73	14.1	545,094	1.4	914	19.9	6,514,436	10.6
1,000,000 - 5,000,000	6,856	52.7	19,687,119	8.1	33	6.4	105,006	0.3	1,687	36.7	4,633,829	7.6
Less than 1,000,000	1,234	9.5	1,014,890	0.4	3	0.6	1,965	*	470	10.2	261,389	0.4
Total	12,998	100.0%	$242,579,820	100.0%	519	100.0%	$38,657,462	100.0%	4,599	100.0%	$53,206,717	100.0%

[1] Deposit size in case of commercial banks.
[2] Data for July 1, 1959.
* Less than 1/10th of 1 percent.

Sources: Federal Deposit Insurance Corporation, Federal Home Loan Bank Board, National Association of Mutual Savings Banks.

14

88 in number and held $28 billion or over 71 percent of the total assets of all mutual savings banks.

At savings and loan associations, a lesser degree of concentration existed. Institutions holding assets in excess of $100 million numbered 71, or 1.5 percent of all associations and held only 21 percent of the total assets of the entire business. Associations exceeding $50 million in assets numbered 227 and held 38 percent of total assets. Thus, the concentration of assets is far less pronounced at savings associations than at banks. The trend at all three types of institutions, however, is toward greater concentration.

TABLE 2-4
Percentage Distribution of Savings in Deposit-type Institutions by Region
December 31, 1959

Region	Commercial Banks[1]	Mutual Savings Banks	Total Banks	Savings and Loan Associations
New England	3.7%	10.5%	5.8%	5.1%
Middle Atlantic	24.5	84.1	43.1	16.7
South Atlantic	8.4	2.5	6.6	14.3
East North Central	25.3	0.4	17.5	27.1
East South Central	3.6	0.0	2.5	3.5
West North Central	7.5	1.1	5.5	8.0
West South Central	5.4	0.0	3.7	6.3
Mountain	3.3	0.0	2.3	3.0
Pacific	18.3	1.4	13.0	16.0
Total	100.0%	100.0%	100.0%	100.0%

[1] Time deposits of individuals, partnerships, and corporations.

Sources: Federal Deposit Insurance Corporation, National Association of Mutual Savings Banks, United States Savings and Loan League.

An analysis of the distribution of savings on a geographic basis by type of institution appears in Table 2-4. In commercial and mutual savings banks combined, over 50 percent of savings deposits can be found in the New England and mid-Atlantic regions. By contrast, only 22 percent of savings and loan savings are in institutions located in those areas. The trend over the past few years, furthermore, has been for a continually smaller proportion of savings and loan savings to be found in the regions east of the Allegheny Mountains with an increasing proportion to be found west of the Mississippi. The only broad regions where savings and loan savings are clearly larger in relation to combined bank time and savings deposits are in the East North Central and South Atlantic regions. Over 14 percent of savings and loan savings are in institutions in the South Atlantic states, stretching from Maryland to Florida, compared with only 6 percent of bank deposits.

Regional Distribution of Assets. In all sections of the country, savings

and loan assets now are many times greater than they were in 1950. The
percentage increase in savings and loan assets by region, 1950 to 1960, is
shown in Table 2-5. Gains were the strongest in the Pacific and Mountain
states and most moderate in the New England and Mid-Atlantic states.
For the nation as a whole, the increase in assets was 323 percent, or 15.6

TABLE 2-5
Growth of Savings and Loan Associations
By Region
1950-1960

Region	Total Assets (Millions of Dollars) 1950	Total Assets (Millions of Dollars) 1960	Percent Increase	Average Annual Rate of Growth (Percent)
New England	$ 1,390	$ 3,437	147%	9.6%
Middle-Atlantic	3,268	11,575	254	13.4
South Central	2,160	10,185	372	16.8
East North Central	4,945	18,974	284	14.4
East South Central	532	2,400	351	16.2
West North Central	1,297	5,701	340	16.1
West South Central	918	4,514	292	17.4
Mountain	409	2,131	421	18.1
Pacific	1,966	12,572	539	20.4
United States	$16,885	$71,489	323%	15.6%

Source: United States Savings and Loan League.

TABLE 2-6
Analysis of Savings and Loan Association Offices
by Location
United States and Possessions
December 31, 1955

1. Number of savings and loan association offices—location by size of urban place,
   1950 Census:

Urban Places	Number of Offices Total	Number of Offices Main	Number of Offices Branch
Less than 10,000 population	1,579	1,485	94
10,000 - 24,999 population	971	882	89
25,000 - 99,999 population	982	892	90
100,000 and over population	2,275	2,026	249
Unclassified areas	883	786	97
Total	6,690	6,071	619

2. Number of urban places in which no savings and loan association office is located:

Urban Places with Population of 10,000 – 24,999	Urban Places with Population of 25,000 - 99,999	Urban Places with Population of 100,000 or More
151	17	None

Source: Federal Home Loan Bank Board.

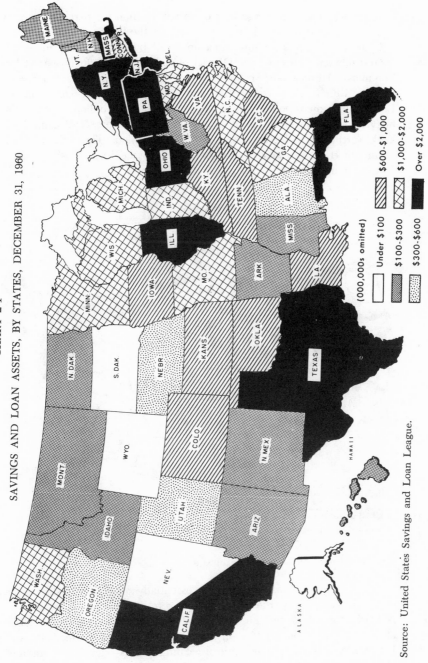

CHART 2-1

SAVINGS AND LOAN ASSETS, BY STATES, DECEMBER 31, 1960

(000,000s omitted)

Under $100

$100-$300

$300-$600

$600-$1,000

$1,000-$2,000

Over $2,000

Source: United States Savings and Loan League.

17

percent per year. The range in growth varied from 9.6 percent per year in New England to 20.4 percent per year on the Pacific Coast.

Chart 2-1 presents savings and loan assets by states on December 31, 1960. Eighteen states and the District of Columbia contained over $1 billion in association assets. Six states reported $3 billion or more: California, Florida, Illinois, New York, Ohio, and Pennsylvania. Associations in the Los Angeles metropolitan area, with assets of $7.1 billion, showed the heaviest local concentration of savings and loan dollars. Next came New York-Northeastern New Jersey, with $5.8 billion. Three-fifths of all savings and loan resources can be found in the forty most populous metropolitan areas.

CHART 2-2

PRIMARY LENDING AREAS OF INSURED SAVINGS
AND LOAN ASSOCIATIONS,
JUNE 30, 1956

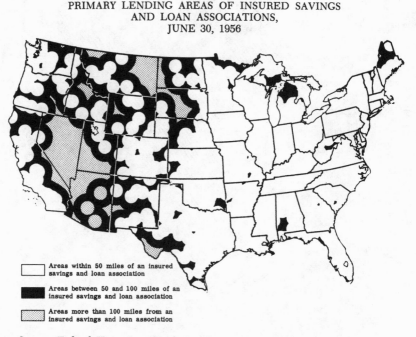

Areas within 50 miles of an insured savings and loan association

Areas between 50 and 100 miles of an insured savings and loan association

Areas more than 100 miles from an insured savings and loan association

Source: Federal Home Loan Bank Board.

The savings and loan business is essentially an urban business; the larger the community, the more likely it is to have a savings association. A study conducted by the Federal Home Loan Bank Board in 1956 of all savings and loan offices in the United States and possessions as of December 31, 1955, proved quite revealing in this regard. The findings of the study indicate that there were no urban areas with 100,000 or more people which did not have a savings association office (Table 2-6).

With the exception of certain sparsely settled areas in the western part of the United States, practically all sections of the country come within the primary legal lending areas of existing insured savings and loan associations (Chart 2-2).

Regional data can be analyzed from another viewpoint. Table 2-7 shows the regional distribution of savings at all savings and loan associations on a percentage basis for the years 1949 to 1960. The relative share of savings in the various sections of the country remained fairly constant over the decade except in the coastal areas. The New England and Mid-Atlantic states have become relatively less important in the savings and loan picture, while the Pacific Coast has risen in prominence. In New England, savings and loan savings have declined from 8.7 percent to 4.9 percent of the national total; in the Mid-Atlantic states, from 19.7 percent to 16.4 percent. On the West Coast, associations have increased their relative share of savings and loan savings from 10.8 percent to 17.0 percent of the total. The South Atlantic area also reported a gain, from 12.5 percent in 1949 to 14.3 percent in 1959.

TABLE 2-7
Percentage Distribution of
Total Savings and Loan Association Savings
By Region
1949–1960

Region	1949	1950	1951	1952	1953	1954	1955	1956	1957	1958	1959	1960
New England	8.7%	8.4%	8.0%	7.5%	7.2%	6.7%	6.3%	5.9%	5.7%	5.4%	5.1%	4.9%
Middle Atlantic	19.7	19.6	19.6	19.2	18.8	18.6	18.2	17.8	17.5	17.0	16.7	16.4
South Atlantic	12.5	12.8	13.2	13.3	13.6	13.8	14.0	14.1	14.3	14.2	14.3	14.3
East North Central	29.6	29.3	29.2	28.9	28.6	28.1	28.0	27.8	27.6	27.5	27.1	26.3
East South Central	3.3	3.3	3.3	3.3	3.3	3.4	3.4	3.4	3.4	3.5	3.5	3.5
West North Central	7.8	7.7	7.2	7.7	7.7	7.9	8.0	8.1	7.9	8.0	8.0	8.2
West South Central	5.3	5.5	5.5	5.9	5.7	5.8	5.9	5.8	6.0	6.1	6.3	6.4
Mountain	2.3	2.3	2.4	2.4	2.5	2.7	2.8	2.9	2.9	3.0	3.0	3.0
Pacific	10.8	11.1	11.6	11.8	12.6	13.0	13.4	14.2	14.7	15.4	16.0	17.0
	100.0%	100.0%	100.0%	100.0%	100.0%	100.0%	100.0%	100.0%	100.0%	100.0%	100.0%	100.0%

Source: United States Savings and Loan League.

TABLE 2-8
Savings and Loan History
Chronology

Year

c. 1780 British building societies appear.

1831 Organization meeting of thirty-seven members of the Oxford Provident Building Association, Frankford, Pennsylvania; adoption of constitution.

1832 First loan made by Oxford Provident Building Society.

1836 Brooklyn Building and Mutual Loan Association organized.

1849 Connecticut passes law making "savings and loan association" the designation of these societies.

1875 New York State requires associations to file annual reports of condition.

1888 First statistical study of associations estimates number of associations at 3,000 to 3,500, with assets of $300 million.

1892 Formation of the United States League of Local Building and Loan Associations, now the United States Savings and Loan League.

1931 All states but two have some degree of regulation over savings and loan associations.

1932 Federal Home Loan Bank System established.

1933 Legislation passed providing for federal savings and loan associations.

1934 Federal Savings and Loan Insurance Corporation (FSLIC) established.

1937 Passage of the United States Housing Act creating the public housing program.

1941 President's National Emergency Proclamation puts economy on virtual war-time basis, restricting construction materials and location of construction.

Federal Reserve Board's Regulation W limits consumer credit.

1942 National Housing Agency formed. Federal Home Loan Bank Board abolished; duties assumed by Federal Home Loan Bank Administration.

Construction Conservation Order L-41 puts savings and loan associations virtually out of construction lending for the duration of the war.

Last exemption of savings and loan dividend payments from federal income tax revoked.

1944 Passage of Servicemen's Readjustment Act creating GI loan program.

1946 Savings and loan assets exceed $10 billion.

1947 Housing and Home Finance Agency created, with responsibility for most agencies supervised by National Housing Agency, which was dissolved.

1949 Retirement of last government capital invested in savings and loan shares.

Adoption of Charter N giving federal associations additional means of raising capital.

1950 Federal Reserve Board Regulation X, authorized under Defense Production Act, brings terms of conventional mortgage lending under government regulation for first time.

Passage of Savings and Loan Act and legislation improving FSLIC.

1951 Federal Home Loan Bank System becomes fully member-owned.

Passage of Revenue Act of 1951 repealing associations' exemption from corporate income tax.

1958 Retirement of last of FSLIC's original government capital.

1961 Savings and loan assets pass $80 billion.

Chapter 3

LEGAL ORGANIZATION

Dual System of Charters

The charter under which an association operates is a contract between the governing authority and the association. Savings and loan associations may be formed under either federal charter or state charter. The charter itself may be long or short, detailed or general, depending upon the state laws or federal statutes under which the association is operating. An analysis of lending powers of federal associations appears in Table 3-1.

State authorities were the only agencies granting association charters prior to 1933. In that year the Home Owners Loan Act provided for the incorporation of federal savings and loan associations under the administration of the Federal Home Loan Bank Board.

State Charters

The typical state charter is brief and simple. It usually includes no more than the name of the association, the purpose of its formation, its place of business, the names and residences of its members and the initial amount of savings capital which each possesses, the duration of the charter, and the number, names, and residences of directors, and their tenure of office. Amendments to a charter may be made by vote of the association members with the approval of the state supervisory authorities. Changes in association name and in the number of directors are the most common amendments.

Incorporation procedures may vary from state to state. Today, practically all states have come to recognize savings and home financing institutions through savings and loan codes enacted to deal with this particular type of financial corporation. Under various codes, states grant powers, rights, and privileges, outline duties and responsibilities, and clarify many details of operation and supervision. These codes pertain to the organization, administration, supervision, and possible liquidation or merging of associations.

The United States Savings and Loan League has evolved a "model code" based on the best features of existing state codes and the considered judgment of leaders in the business.[1] In recent years the act has been adopted in substance by the legislatures of Alaska, Arizona, Iowa, Maine, and Missouri, and is presently under consideration in at least ten other states.

Federal Charters

The establishment of federal savings and loan associations was authorized by the Home Owners' Loan Act of 1933. Section 5 (a) of this Act states:

> In order to provide local mutual thrift institutions in which people may invest their funds and in order to provide for the financing of homes, the Board is authorized, under such rules and regulations as it may prescribe, to provide for the organization, incorporation, examination, operation and regulation of associations to be known as "Federal Savings and Loan Associations" and to issue charters therefore, giving primary consideration to the best practices of local mutual thrift and home financing institutions in the United States.

The original regulations, including the original charter form (Charter E), were promulgated in that year. This plan of organization promoted stability and uniformity of savings associations by providing for federally chartered savings associations throughout the country. Although the federal charter and regulations were a considerable improvement over most state laws and regulations, there were still some shortcomings in the early charters. The original Charter E provided for four different kinds of accounts, retained certain undesirable withdrawal penalties, and utilized much of the confusing terminology of the 1920's.

In 1936, the rules and regulations for establishing federal savings and loan associations were comprehensively revised, and a new charter form (Charter K) was authorized. The new charter form provided for only two types of accounts—savings accounts and investment accounts—and was adopted by nearly all federal associations.

Another comprehensive revision of the regulations and charter was undertaken in 1949. Its objective was to simplify the regulations and the charter and to provide greater flexibility in savings association operations than was permitted under Charter K. The proposed charter (Charter N) was much shorter than the previous charters and used modern terminology. It also was substantially different in form and substance; it was a mere franchise to do business, and it transferred the provisions for

---

[1] By writing to the U. S. Savings and Loan League, those interested may secure a copy of the Model Savings and Loan Act which appeared in the League's *Legal Bulletin* (January 1961).

TABLE 3-1
Lending Powers of Federal Savings and Loan Associations under Various Charters
Charters N and K (Rev.) Associations

Type of Loan	Max. Term of Years	Interest Payments Mo. or Max. Interval	Principal Payments	20% of Assets Limit (Within 50-Mile Radius or req. lend. area)	20% of Assets Limit (Outside 50-Mile Radius or req. lend. area)	Maximum Loan-To-Value Ratio	Directors May Authorize
SAVINGS ACCOUNT LOANS				No	No	100% of withdrawal value	
FIRST MTGE. HOME AND COMB. HOME AND BUSINESS							
Monthly instalment	25	Monthly	Monthly	No, except if over $35,000	Yes	75%	80% / 80%
Other Instalment	5	Semi-An.	Regular at least annually	No, except if over $35,000	Yes		80%
Other Instalment	15	Semi-An.	Maturity	Yes	Yes	50%	80%
Non-Instalment	5	Semi-An.	Maturity	Yes	Yes		50%
Non-Instalment	3	Semi-An.	Maturity	Yes	Yes		60%
Non-Instalment (constr. only)	1	Semi-An.	Maturity	Yes	Yes		80%
Instalment (one-family, completed residence; loan must be for *purchase* of property; Assn. must have 3% reserves; sales, participations barred. Const. loan to vendor apvd.; pay-outs over 80%-of-value barred until completion, sale and assumption.)	25	Monthly, plus tax and insurance pymts. in advance	Monthly	No, but these loans in aggregate limited to 15% of savings. 15%-limit dropped on loans paid down to 80%	Yes	The least of: (1) 90% of first $20,000 of value of real estate plus 80% of the next $5,000 of value (2) 90% of first $20,000 of certified purchase price plus 80% of the next $5,000 of such price or (3) $22,000. Directors may authorize.	
VA Loans		Acceptable to the VA		No, if 20% gtd.	No, if 20% gtd. loan is made or purchased		80% plus gty.
FHA Loans		Acceptable to the FHA		No	Yes, if loan is made; no if purchased		Acceptable to FHA.
FIRST MTGE.—"OTHER IMPROVED REAL ESTATE" (Income Producing)							
5-6 Family Residences	25	Monthly	Monthly	Yes	Yes	50%	75%
	5	Semi-An.	Maturity	Yes	Yes	50%	50%
	3	Semi-An.	Maturity	Yes	Yes		60%
7-12 Family Residences	25*	Monthly	Monthly	Yes	Yes	50%	60%
	20*	Monthly	Monthly	Yes	Yes		70%
	5	Semi-An.	Maturity	Yes	Yes	50%	50%
	3	Semi-An.	Maturity	Yes	Yes		60%
Primarily Residential for 6 Families and Under	25	Monthly	Monthly	Yes	Yes	50%	50%
	15*	Monthly	Monthly	Yes	Yes	50%	66⅔%
	5	Semi-An.	Maturity	Yes	Yes		50%
	3	Semi-An.	Maturity	Yes	Yes		60%

Primarily Residential for Over 6 Families	25*	Monthly	Monthly	Yes	Yes	50%	50%
	20*	Monthly	Monthly	Yes	Yes	-	70%
	5	Semi-An.	Maturity	Yes	Yes	50%	50%
	3	Semi-An.	Maturity	Yes	Yes	-	60%
Business Property	25	Monthly	Monthly	Yes	Yes	50%	50%
	20	Monthly	Monthly	Yes	Yes	-	60%
	5	Semi-An.	Maturity	Yes	Yes	50%	50%
FHA Loans	Acceptable to the FHA			Yes	Yes	-	Acceptable to FHA.
VA Loans	Acceptable to the VA			No, if 20%-gtd.	No, if 20%-gtd. loan is made or purchased		% of value above plus amount of gty. prov. any % may be loaned if 20% gtd.
FIRST MTGE.—"OTHER IMPROVED REAL ESTATE" (Developed Sites) Developed sites for 1-family structures; constr. must begin in 6 months, completion within 3 yrs.	3	Semi-An.	Maturity	Yes; total such loans also subject to special 5%-of-assets limit. Must be within reg. lending area.	No, but total such loans subject to special 5%-of-withdrawable-accts. limit. Must be within reg. lending area.		70%. Aggregate loan balances to any "applicant" not to exceed 1%-of-assets.
FIRST MTGE.—LAND ACQUISITION AND DEVELOPMENT Primarily Residential. (Assn. must have 5% of withdrawable accts. in reserves and undiv. profits; sales, purchases, participations barred.)	3	Semi-An.	Maturity				The least of (1) 60% of the value of r.e. as a completed project or (2) 60% of value of r.e. at time loan is made plus 60% of cost of development. Aggregate loan balances to any "applicant" not to exceed 20% of 5%-of-withdrawable-accts.

PARTICIPATING INTERESTS: (1) May participate with U.S. instrumentalities, FDIC- and FSLIC-insured lenders in making or purchase of loans *within* regular lending area of a type assn. may otherwise make, the Sec. 545.6-7 20%-of-assets-limit applying only where applicable for a reason other than the participation aspect; (2) May participate with FSLIC-insured lenders in making or purchase of 1-4 family home loans *outside* regular lending area, but these participations may not exceed amount equal to the difference between 30%-of-assets and the amount of all loans and participations falling in Sec. 545.6-7 20%-of-assets-limit. Participations in FHA or VA loans not counted in either of above categories.

SECOND MTGE. LOANS Guaranteed VA Loans	Acceptable to the VA			No, if 20% gtd.	No, if 20% gtd.		Only if 20% gtd.
UNSECURED LOANS Guaranteed VA Loans	Acceptable to the VA			Special 15% of Assets Limit			Only if evidenced by note, and within regular lending area.
Property Improvement	5	Monthly	Monthly				Only if $3500 or under, evidenced by note, and within regular lending area.
FHA Property Improvement	Acceptable to the FHA						Only if evidenced by note, and within regular lending area.
VA-Insured Prop. Imp. VA-Gteed. Prop. Impr. when Gty. under 20%.	Acceptable to the VA						Only if evidenced by note, and within regular lending area.

25

*May be 25 years when "government entity" certifies in advance that development, alteration, repair, or improvement of the property is in connection with the objectives of a slum clearance or urban renewal program by such entity.

(Continued)

TABLE 3-1 (Continued)

Charter K (with Sec. 14.1) Associations

Type of Loan	Max. Term of Years	Interest Payments Mo. or Max. Interval	Principal Payments	20% of Assets Limit (Within 50-Mile Radius or req. lend. area)	20% of Assets Limit (Outside 50-Mile Radius or req. lend. area)	Maximum Loan-To-Value Ratio	Directors May Authorize
SAVINGS ACCOUNT LOANS				No	No	90% of Repurchase value	
FIRST MTGE. – HOME AND COMB. HOME AND BUSINESS Monthly instalment	25	Monthly	Monthly	No, except if over $35,000	Yes	75%	80%
Other Instalment	5	Semi-An.	Regular at least annually	No, except if over $35,000	Yes		80%
Other Instalment	15	Semi-An.	,,	Yes	Yes		80%
Non-Instalment	5	Semi-An.	Maturity	Yes	Yes	50%	50%
Non-Instalment	3	Semi-An.	Maturity	Yes	Yes		60%
Non-Instalment (constr. only)	1	Semi-An.	Maturity	Yes	Yes		80%
Instalment (one-family, completed residence; loan must be for *purchase* of property; Assn. must have 3% reserves; sales, participations barred. Constr. loan to vendor apvd; pay-outs over 80%-of-value barred until completion, sale and assumption.)	25	Monthly, plus tax and insurance pymts. in advance	Monthly	No, but these loans in aggregate limited to 15% of savings. 15% limit dropped on loans paid down to 80%.	Yes	50%	The least of: (1) 90% of first $20,000 of value of real estate plus 80% of the next $5,000 of value, (2) 90% of first $20,000 of certified purchase price plus 80% of the next $5,000 of such price, or (3) $22,000. Directors may authorize.
VA Loans	Acceptable to the VA		No, if 20%-gtd.	No, if 20%-gtd. loan is made or purchased.		80% plus gty.
FHA Loans	Acceptable to the FHA		No	Yes, if loan is made; no if purchased.		Acceptable to FHA.
FIRST MTGE. – "OTHER IMPROVED REAL ESTATE" (Income producing) 5-6 Family Residences	25	Monthly	Monthly	Yes	Yes	50%	75%
	5	Semi-An.	Maturity	Yes	Yes	50%	50%
	3	Semi-An.	Maturity	Yes	Yes		60%
7-12 Family Residences	25	Monthly	Monthly	Yes	Yes	50%	60%
	20*	Monthly	Monthly	Yes	Yes		70%
	5	Semi-An.	Maturity	Yes	Yes	50%	50%
	3	Semi-An.	Maturity	Yes	Yes		60%

Category	Maturity (yrs)						
Primarily Residential for 6 Families and Under	25	Monthly	Monthly	Yes	Yes	50%	50%
	15*	Monthly	Monthly	Yes	Yes		66⅔%
	5	Semi-An.	Maturity	Yes	Yes	50%	50%
	3	Semi-An.	Maturity	Yes	Yes		60%
Primarily Residential for Over 6 Families	25	Monthly	Monthly	Yes	Yes	50%	50%
	20*	Monthly	Monthly	Yes	Yes		70%
	5	Semi-An.	Maturity	Yes	Yes	50%	50%
	3	Semi-An.	Maturity	Yes	Yes		60%
Business Property	25	Monthly	Monthly	Yes	Yes	50%	50%
	20	Monthly	Monthly	Yes	Yes		60%
	5	Semi-An.	Maturity	Yes	Yes	50%	50%
FHA Loans		Acceptable to the FHA		Yes	Yes		Acceptable to FHA.
VA Loans		Acceptable to the VA		No, if 20% gtd.	No, if 20%-gtd. loan is made or purchased.		% of value above plus amount of gty. prov., any % may be loaned if 20% gtd.
SECOND MTGE. LOANS Guaranteed VA Loans		Acceptable to the VA		No, if 20% gtd.	No, if 20% gtd.		Only if 20% gtd.
UNSECURED LOANS Guaranteed VA Loans		Acceptable to the VA					Only if evidenced by note, and within regular lending area.
Property Improvement	5	Monthly	Monthly	Special 15% of Assets Limit			Only if $3500 or under, evidenced by note, and within regular lending area.
FHA Property Improvement		Acceptable to the FHA					Only if evidenced by note, and within regular lending area.
VA-Insured Prop. Imp.; VA-Gteed. Prop. Imp. when Gty. under 20%.		Acceptable to the VA					Only if evidenced by note, and within regular lending area.

PARTICIPATING INTERESTS: (1) May participate with U.S. instrumentalities, FDIC- and FSLIC-insured lenders in making or purchase of loans *within* regular lending area of a type assn. may otherwise make, the Sec. 545.6-7 20%-of-assets-limit applying only where applicable for a reason other than the participation aspect; (2) May participate with FSLIC-insured lenders in making or purchase of 1-4 family home loans *outside* regular lending area, but these participations may not exceed amount equal to the difference between 30%-of-assets and the amount of all loans and participations falling in Sec. 545.6-7 20%-of-assets-limit. Participations in FHA or VA loans not counted in either of above categories.

27

*May be 25 years when "government entity" certifies in advance that development, alteration, repair, or improvement of the property is in connection with the objectives of a slum clearance or urban renewal program by such entity.

**Chart applies also to Charter K associations which have not added Sec. 14.1 to their charters, excepting that maximum percentages in far-right column must be authorized, not by directors, but by the members.

practically all the corporate powers and procedures from the charter to the regulations of the Federal Home Loan Bank Board.

The United States Savings and Loan League, supported by many state leagues, urged numerous changes in the proposed charter, most of them for the protection of local savings and loan management and savings association members. Among other things, it urged that corporate powers and procedures be retained in the charter. Except for one provision relative to withdrawal rules, these recommendations were embodied in the final draft of Charter N, issued in 1949. The excepted provision was included in a later charter form, Charter K (Revised),[2] which is identical to Charter N, except that it permits including the provisions relative to the withdrawal arrangement, rather than having them prescribed by regulation, as was the case under Charter N.[3] (Since the several forms of federal charters contain varying provisions, the particular provisions under which an association is operating can be determined by reference to its charter.)

A savings and loan association can be subject to one or more of four general systems of regulatory control or influence: Federal Savings and Loan System, Federal Savings and Loan Insurance System, Federal Home Loan Bank System, and/or an appropriate state regulatory system.

State-chartered institutions operate under various laws and regulations which in some cases parallel those of the federal system, in some cases are more restrictive, and in still others less stringent. Some idea of the variations in state laws can be gleaned from Appendix A, which summarizes provisions of state statutes covering maximum ratio of loan to value, maximum maturity of the conventional mortgage loan, and maximum amount of loan.

The legal framework through which savings and loans operate in a specific state and the legal conditions facing associations in a state, can have a bearing on the growth record of the business. Certain lenders consider investments in mortgages in specific states relatively unattractive because of legal restrictions such as lengthy redemption privileges granted to homeowners or strict usury laws at a relatively low ceiling. The result of such provisions can be to leave local markets to local lenders. Where such conditions exist in rapidly growing localities such

---

[2] The regulations promulgated by the Board in 1953 automatically gave the Board's authorization to Charter N, Charter K, and Charter E associations to adopt Charter K (Revised). New associations may be organized under either Charter N or Charter K (Revised).

[3] Section VI of Charter N provides simply that withdrawals will be met as stipulated in the regulations, whereas Charter K and Charter K (Revised) provide a definite withdrawal contract which can be changed only upon the consent of the members as well as of the Federal Home Loan Bank Board. The withdrawal arrangements for Charter N associations, stated in the regulations and not in the association Charter, could be changed by the Board without the consent of the association.

as the Chicago metropolitan area, savings associations find their lending opportunities relatively greater than would be the case elsewhere because large eastern insurance companies consider foreclosure laws in Illinois quite restrictive.[4]

Delegation of Powers

Even though the members of an incorporated mutual association are its owners, it is not practicable for them to manage the business themselves. A representative form of corporate government is necessary, under which the owners delegate the actual management to directors and officers. The control by savings account holders and borrowers is limited to a set of rules which the members prescribe for the selection and instruction of their representatives, to resolutions which the members may pass to guide their representatives, and to the election of directors at the annual membership meetings. The rules through which the managing board is selected and governed are known as the bylaws of the association. Included in the bylaws are provisions for the time of annual meeting, number of directors, issuance of various classes or types of savings accounts, types of lending plans, method of distributing earnings, and the duties, obligations, and responsibilities of the elected and appointed officers.

Effect on Savings and Loan Growth and Entry

The growth of savings and loan associations is directly related to the legal and regulatory provisions pertaining to such institutions. Some of the laws and regulations affecting associations may be considered favorable to their growth; others may be considered to have retarded it. Generally, the set of statutes or regulations under which savings and loan associations operate are workable.

The dual system of charters has an advantage from the viewpoint of checks and balances. Federal regulatory agencies and the various state agencies seem to a degree to compete with each other. Individual institutions thus have some ability at times to play one chartering agency against another and to introduce innovations into their operations more readily than they could if only a single chartering system existed.

Entry into the savings and loan business is regulated by state and federal agencies, just as is entry into the banking business. In the case of federal charters, four general tests were established by the Home Owners Loan Act of 1933. These are:

---

[4] A comprehensive study of the investment powers of savings and loan associations on a state-by-state basis was prepared by the United States League's Legal Department and published in its *Legal Bulletin* (January 1956). Copies of this report are available from the League upon request.

1) The good character and responsibility of each member of the applicant group,

2) The existence of a need for a federal association in the community to be served,

3) The reasonable probability of the usefulness and success of a new association so located,

4) Whether such federal association can be established without causing undue injury to properly conducted, existing local thrift and home financing institutions.

The amount of savings capital which is required for the establishment of an association varies with the circumstances. A group seeking a charter in a relatively sparsely settled area where competition is limited may find its capital requirement to be $200,000. In a highly competitive urban market the requirement might run to a million dollars. The chartering agencies are given broad discretion in the authorizing of new institutions.[5]

The examining and regulating authorities appear to be fairly well imbued with the philosophy of savings associations as local, home financing institutions. They have had little or no inclination to broaden the lending powers of associations to include elements other than those tied to the shelter requirements of the American people. Even in the savings aspect of the business, the regulations adopted can be interpreted as having their motivation in a desire to serve the home financing needs of the American people and to fulfill the home financing responsibilities placed on associations by the federal agencies. Restrictions on the powers of savings associations, especially on the lending side, might be considered serious drawbacks by casual observers. The geographic lending area, the types of dwellings on which mortgage loans may be made, the services which may be offered to the public, and the types of accounts which may be held all are restricted. The specific types of lending which may be undertaken by federal savings and loan associations under the various charters—Charter K, Charter N, and Charter K (Revised)—are listed in Table 3-1.

Suggested Statute Changes

There are a number of changes in the statutes and regulations affecting savings and loan associations which would permit them to accomplish more effectively their mission of providing for the shelter requirements of the American people within the framework of private financial institutions:

1) *Trade-in housing.* Extending the lending authority of savings and

---

[5] Most Federal Home Loan Banks have prepared brochures outlining the manner in which new federal associations might be organized. Copies of such materials should be available through the regional Banks.

loan associations to include the acceptance of existing dwelling units as security for short-term advances would facilitate the transfer of property from one owner to another. Such authority already exists in several states for state-chartered institutions.

2) *Right to sell participations in home mortgage loans (up to 75 percent of individual loans) to pension funds.* This power would enable pension funds to participate in local mortgage lending activities without incurring the burden of originating and servicing the individual loan contracts.

3) *More liberal terms on multi-family property loans.* Present restrictions on the lending activity of savings and loan associations in the area of multi-family dwellings are stricter than for single-family units. To serve the housing needs of the growing number of young married families and elderly individuals, a great number of multi-family properties may have to be built in the years ahead, and associations ought to be able to participate in this area more freely than is possible under current regulations.

4) *Secondary mortgage market facility.* Creation of a secondary market facility, within the framework of the Federal Home Loan Bank System, which could buy and sell loans from and to individual member institutions would enhance the mobility of home mortgages. Such a facility should also have the right to issue debentures in the capital markets so that additional funds could be channeled to member institutions working in the support of home ownership.

5) *Power to invest in municipal obligations to build facilities for new neighborhoods.* One of the continuing problems facing home building is the financing of municipal improvements in new housing areas. Savings and loan associations, if given the power, might well provide a sizable pool of funds to support such neighborhood projects through purchase of municipal obligations floated with this purpose in mind. In this regard, associations are not interested in purchasing general obligations of states or municipalities, but rather specific issues raising funds to meet the broader aspects of the shelter requirements of the American people.

Chapter 4

COMPETITION AND GROWTH

Competition Within the Business

Savings and loan associations are essentially local institutions, competing with other institutions in the immediate area for savings funds with which to make mortgage loans. Although a number of institutions solicit savings nationally, they are the exception, and even they find the bulk of their money coming from their own localities.

The penetration of the savings markets by associations in individual states and metropolitan areas provides some indication of the local import of the savings and loan business. Table 4-1 shows the per capita assets of savings associations by state at the end of 1960. There is not necessarily a direct relationship between the per capita assets of associations and the per capita income of individuals. The South Dakota–North Dakota picture is a case in point. On the basis of per capita income the two states were quite similar, yet, in South Dakota, savings and loan assets averaged $125 per person, while in North Dakota they amounted to $313 per person. Michigan and Ohio are other neighboring states where per capita income was comparable, but where a considerable discrepancy existed in per capita savings and loan assets. In Ohio, per capita assets at $681 were the second highest in the nation, while in Michigan, association assets of $242 per person were well below the national average. Per capita income of $2,328 in Ohio in 1959 was $75 higher than in Michigan. The reasons for the variation must be tied to factors other than income of residents.

Competition for Savings

Competition for savings among associations varies from place to place. There seems to be no criteria for determining the degree of competition one might expect to find from one city to the next. Custom and tradition, the number of institutions in a particular market area, and attitudes toward the promotion of savings are among the determinants of intra-

32

TABLE 4-1
Per Capita Savings and Loan Assets
by State
December 31, 1960

State	Per Capita Assets	State	Per Capita Assets
Alabama	$ 143	Montana	$ 191
Alaska	66	Nebraska	322
Arizona	206	Nevada	333
Arkansas	167	New Hampshire	264
California	679	New Jersey	464
Colorado	476	New Mexico	184
Connecticut	277	New York	287
Delaware	119	North Carolina	303
District of Columbia	1,688	North Dakota	313
Florida	653	Ohio	681
Georgia	276	Oklahoma	314
Hawaii	325	Oregon	263
Idaho	273	Pennsylvania	348
Illinois	681	Rhode Island	312
Indiana	396	South Carolina	273
Iowa	284	South Dakota	125
Kansas	381	Tennessee	204
Kentucky	299	Texas	293
Louisiana	296	Utah	326
Maine	108	Vermont	115
Maryland	492	Virginia	169
Massachusetts	419	Washington	453
Michigan	242	West Virginia	112
Minnesota	448	Wisconsin	448
Mississippi	137	Wyoming	248
Missouri	355	ENTIRE U.S.	399

Source: United States Savings and Loan League.

industry competition on the savings side. Where competition for savings has been most intense, it has taken the form of concentrated merchandising efforts, such as aggressive promotion of the rate of return available to savers, giveaway campaigns, and the like.

It has become almost axiomatic among savings and loan managers that individual institutions wishing to retain their savings accounts and to continue to grow must not permit competing institutions in their market area to offer a rate of return on savings higher than their own. As a consequence, the rate of return offered by individual institutions in a particular market area tends to be quite similar; the savings product of competing associations is therefore identical in the eyes of the typical saver. Federal insurance of accounts has done much to make this so.

Another rule of thumb commonly held in the savings and loan business is that associations need a 0.5 percent to 1 percent rate advantage over commercial banks, apparently to compensate savers for surmounting a psychological hurdle regarding the relative safety and convenience of the two types of institution. Some associations in outlying areas feel that they need a 0.25 percent to 0.5 percent spread over downtown associations because of the inconvenience of their location contrasted to the heavily traveled central section of a city.

The use of premiums and gifts to attract savings and loan accounts has been intensively used by many association managers during the past decade. The practice became so widespread during 1955, and so distasteful to most people in the savings and loan business, that the Federal Home Loan Bank Board was called on to adopt a regulation limiting giveaways to merchandise costing not more than $2.50 per account. There is little doubt among savings and loan practitioners that an appropriate premium, aggressively promoted, can bring in considerable funds for a savings association.

Competition for Mortgage Loans

The growth of lending by the savings and loan business has been due to the rising demand for its services and its increasing share of the total market. Since the end of World War II, savings associations have benefited from (and have helped make possible) the record demand for new homes and the record volume of real estate activity which accompanied this home building.

Competition for mortgages among savings and loans intensified throughout the 1950's and continues to grow. In general, the greater the share of the lending market secured by associations, the greater the competition among associations themselves. The reason for this is simple. During the early postwar period, before savings associations reached their present level of mortgage-market penetration, their major competition for loans came from insurance companies and mortgage bankers. Throughout the 1950's, however, associations increased their share of the mortgage lending market in city after city. The least efficient mortgage lenders were squeezed out of the area, leaving only the more efficient and aggressive lenders in the market. More often than not, savings and loan associations became the primary lending institution. As efficient, local, specialized home financing institutions, they are able to provide fast, tailor-made loan service at competitive prices. The proportion of mortgage loans recorded by savings associations in selected metropolitan areas during 1960, along with comparable data for 1950, can be seen in Table 4-2. In many cities the ability of associations to make further gains at the expense of competition is currently more limited than it was during the postwar years. Associations find their most aggressive competition no longer comes from mortgage bankers and insurance companies, but from other savings and loan associations.

Competition and Mortgage Rates. Heightened competition may lead

TABLE 4-2
Savings and Loan Proportion of Total Home Mortgage Loans Made, $20,000 or less
Selected Metropolitan Areas
1950-1960

Metropolitan Area	Percentage of Market		Change
	1950	1960	
Akron, Ohio	39.7%	52.2%	+12.5
Atlanta, Ga.	34.6	30.4	− 4.2
Baltimore, Md.	60.7	66.3	+ 5.6
Boston, Mass.	37.1	36.1	− 1.0
Chicago, Ill.	46.3	67.8	+21.5
Cincinnati, Ohio	68.6	77.1	+ 8.5
Dayton, Ohio	58.1	37.3	−20.8
Denver, Colo.	23.0	30.0	+ 7.0
Des Moines, Iowa	51.9	61.3	+ 9.4
Detroit, Mich.	12.6	29.9	+17.3
Indianapolis, Ind.	35.5	41.5	+ 6.0
Milwaukee, Wis.	47.3	55.4	+ 8.1
Minneapolis, Minn.	35.1	52.2	+17.1
New Orleans, La.	44.8	54.4	+ 9.6
New York, N.Y.	25.7	28.0	+ 2.3
Portland, Ore.	21.6	33.7	+12.1
San Diego, Calif.	22.9	41.6	+18.7
San Francisco, Calif.	17.3	46.9	+29.6
Seattle, Wash.	16.4	23.7	+ 7.3

Source: Federal Home Loan Bank Board.

to lower interest rates and benefits for home buyers. Some light can be shed on this question through examination of data on mortgage recordings and interest rates charged on conventional loans. When mortgage recordings by mutual thrift institutions are plotted against interest rates on conventional loans, the following conclusion is suggested: The higher the proportion of the mortgage market served by mutual thrift institutions (savings and loan associations and savings banks), the lower the cost of mortgage funds to borrowers in that area. This finding is supported graphically in Chart 4-1. The technique used was to plot the percentage of home mortgages of $20,000 and less recorded by mutual thrift institutions against the reported conventional lending rate in each state. The data used were mortgage recordings of $20,000 or less (as reported by the Federal Home Loan Bank Board), and interest rates on conventional loans (as reported by home builders and realtors to the Subcommittee on Housing of the House Banking and Currency Committee during late January 1960). Although both sets of data are subject to serious limitations and do not lend themselves to rigorous analysis, the conclusions drawn appear sufficiently broad to stand as stated. Similar analyses were conducted using, in one instance, interest rate data for four-year periods, as supplied by managers of savings and loan associations and, in another instance, quarterly data furnished by regional directors of the Federal Housing Administration. In both cases the general pattern described here holds.

Other hypotheses suggest themselves. Where economic growth and the demand for funds to support that growth run ahead of the ability of the area to accumulate savings, the price of money tends to rise. The high cost of money on the Pacific Coast, where borrowers pay premium

CHART 4-1

MORTGAGE MARKET PENETRATION BY MUTUAL THRIFT INSTITUTIONS AND INTEREST RATES ON CONVENTIONAL LOANS, SELECTED STATES

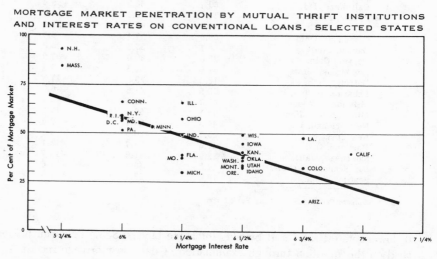

Source: Mortgage Recording, FHLBB, 1959; Interest Rate Survey, 241 builders, 199 realtors replying to Subcommittee on Housing, Committee on Banking and Currency, House of Representatives, February 5, 1960.

rates for home loans, is a case in point. The strong growth of savings associations in the California area may bring the cost of home loans in the Far West closer to the national average. The 6.6 percent and 7.2 percent rates prevailing in California in 1960 are little changed from the rates of 1956 and 1957. Tight money has had less impact on home loans in California than elsewhere. One reason may be that competition among associations has increased, and the pool or supply of funds being directed toward home building demands is larger. The share of mortgage lending attributed to associations in California rose from 35 percent of total mortgage recordings in the state in 1958 to 43 percent in 1960. The California experience may be typical of the problems which come to any business which moves through a vigorous period of growth from an expanding toward a maturing market.

Throughout the history of savings and loans, legal and regulatory measures more often than not have been designed to preserve the local character of the institutions. In order to insure that mortgage money from a local source would be available in just about every section of the country, Congress has restricted savings associations to the home financing function and to the support of home ownership in a relatively limited geographic area. Among the measures adopted with this view in mind are:

1) Limitation of the primary lending area of an association to within fifty miles of its office;

2) Specification that majority of funds be invested in first-mortgage home loans (typically, other investments are limited to 20 percent of total savings);

3) Restrictions as to type and amount of investments which can be made, other than first mortgage loans and government securities;

4) Limitation on ability to buy and sell loans or participations in loans.

More recently, the Federal Home Loan Bank Board adopted a regulation limiting to 5 percent of total savings the amount of funds an association may accept through money brokers, firms which solicit funds from savers (typically those in lower dividend rate areas), and channel them to associations located in higher rate areas which are seeking funds. Although the reasons for the adoption of this regulation are complex, once again the concept of savings associations as regional and local institutions appears to have carried some weight in the deliberations.

The recent loan participation regulations, whereby an association may sell up to 75 percent of its interest in a mortgage to another institution, can be interpreted as a device to permit an association in a local area to meet a sudden spurt in the demand for home financing funds in that area which could not be served from the available savings resources.

Competition with Other Intermediaries

The world of finance is highly competitive. A host of financial institutions vie with each other for a common pool of funds and for a limited number of investment outlets. This is true particularly for the financial intermediaries which do not have among their powers the right to create money and credit. Competition exists for funds (savings) and for investments (loans and securities). Each of the various types of institutions operates under its own set of legal powers, its own customs and traditions, and its own objectives regarding profits and/or service to the American public. In the paragraphs which follow, the competitive positions of savings associations as compared with commercial banks and other financial intermediaries will be explored in detail.

As mentioned previously, savings and loan associations are specialty shops of home financing and thrift. They are essentially local institutions.

Their activities are concentrated in their own locality, and typically they do not cultivate intensively even their entire fifty-mile lending radius. The points of impact with other institutions are in two activities: the market for personal savings and the market for mortgage loans on one- to four-family houses.

Competition for Savings

Defining the competition of savings and loan associations for savings is difficult, to say the least. In the broadest sense, managers recognize that they are in competition for a share of the consumer dollar with General Motors, Ford, General Electric, and any other business enterprise seeking the favor of consumers. They know, too, that they are in competition with the financial institutions of America offering insurance against hazards to person and property, with the pension funds, including the Old Age and Survivors Insurance Fund, with mutual investment funds, and with direct investment by individuals in securities and real estate.

Clean-cut distinctions between institutional savings and other forms of savings are difficult to make. Each definition of "savings" must be adapted to the purpose at hand.[1]

Defining and Measuring Savings

For want of a better term, we call the sector of the savings market in which savings and loan associations are most directly involved, the "over-the-counter savings" market. The over-the-counter savings market is defined as the savings of individuals at commercial banks, savings and loan associations, mutual savings banks and credit unions, in United States savings bonds, and in postal savings. All the institutions have one common characteristic: they offer availability and dollar safety to the saver. Principal funds accepted are returned to savers on a dollar-for-

---

[1] The three principal agencies concerned with developing estimates of aggregate savings volume are the Department of Commerce, the Securities and Exchange Commission, and the Federal Home Loan Bank Board. The Department of Commerce definition involves three steps. From its estimate of total personal income developed through wage and salary data, proprietors' income, and return on investments of individuals, personal taxes are deducted to arrive at disposable personal income. Consumption expenditures, including those made on a credit basis, are then subtracted from disposable personal income and the result is personal savings, a residual figure. The Securities and Exchange Commission includes five types of savings in its definition: currency and deposits (including demand and time accounts), savings at savings and loan associations and credit unions, security issues of corporation and governmental units, private insurance and pension reserves, and state and federal government insurance and pension reserves. From the sum of these amounts the SEC deducts increases in individuals' debts on mortgages, installment obligations, and security loans. The Federal Home Loan Bank Board reports savings of individuals in deposit-type thrift institutions and the change in reserves of life insurance companies. From the savings and loan point of view, the several methods of computing the annual volume of individual savings need not be reconciled.

TABLE 4-3
Savings of Individuals in Selected Media
1947-1960
(Billions of Dollars)

Year	Savings & Loan Assns.	Mutual Savings Banks	Comm'l Banks	Credit Unions	U.S. Savings Bonds	Postal Savings	Total
1947	$ 9.8	$17.7	$34.7	$0.5	$46.2	$3.5	$112.4
1948	11.0	18.4	35.0	0.6	47.8	3.4	116.2
1949	12.5	19.3	35.1	0.7	49.3	3.3	120.2
1950	14.0	20.0	35.2	0.9	49.6	3.0	122.7
1951	16.1	20.9	36.6	1.1	49.1	2.8	126.6
1952	19.2	22.6	39.3	1.4	49.2	2.7	134.4
1953	22.8	24.3	42.0	1.7	49.4	2.5	142.7
1954	27.3	26.3	44.7	2.0	50.0	2.2	152.5
1955	32.2	28.1	46.3	2.4	50.2	2.0	161.2
1956	37.1	30.0	48.5	2.9	50.1	1.7	170.3
1957	41.9	31.7	53.7	3.4	48.2	1.4	180.3
1958	48.0	34.0	60.0	3.9	47.7	1.2	194.8
1959	54.6	34.9	62.9	4.4	45.8	1.0	203.6
1960	62.2	36.3	67.5	4.9	45.3	0.8	217.0

Percentage Distribution

Year	Savings & Loan Assns.	Mutual Savings Banks	Comm'l Banks	Credit Unions	U.S. Savings Bonds	Postal Savings	Total
1947	8.7%	15.7%	30.9%	0.4%	41.2%	3.1%	100.0%
1948	9.5	15.9	30.1	0.5	41.1	2.9	100.0
1949	10.4	16.1	29.2	0.6	41.0	2.7	100.0
1950	11.4	16.3	28.7	0.7	40.4	2.5	100.0
1951	12.7	16.5	28.9	0.9	38.8	2.2	100.0
1952	14.3	16.8	29.2	1.1	36.6	2.0	100.0
1953	16.0	17.0	29.4	1.2	34.6	1.8	100.0
1954	17.9	17.2	29.3	1.3	32.8	1.5	100.0
1955	20.0	17.4	28.7	1.5	31.1	1.3	100.0
1956	21.8	17.6	28.5	1.7	29.4	1.0	100.0
1957	23.2	17.6	29.8	1.9	26.7	0.8	100.0
1958	24.6	17.5	30.8	2.0	24.5	0.6	100.0
1959	26.8	17.1	30.9	2.2	22.5	0.5	100.0
1960	28.7	16.7	31.1	2.3	20.8	0.4	100.0

Source: Federal Home Loan Bank Board.

dollar basis. Taken together, such institutionalized savings are among the fastest growing and largest segments of the savings field. This definition corresponds most closely to the concept adhered to by the Federal Home Loan Bank Board in its report on savings activity, as distinguished from data developed by the SEC or the Department of Commerce.

Of the major financial institutions, savings and loan associations have grown the most rapidly. Total savings rose from less than $10 billion in 1947 to over $62 billion in 1960. Table 4-3 shows the trend in savings at over-the-counter type institutions between 1947 and 1960. On a percentage basis savings and loan associations and credit unions increased their share of the market most markedly. Associations now hold 28.7 percent of over-the-counter savings as compared with only 8.7 percent in

TABLE 4-4
Per Capita Time Deposits at Banks
and Savings at Savings and Loan Associations by State
1950 and 1959

State	Per Capita Savings				Percentage Gain	
	1950		1959			
	Banks*	Assns.	Banks*	Assns.	Banks	Assns.
NEW ENGLAND	$ 793.72	$126.00	$1,156.17	$ 273.80	45.7%	117.3%
Maine	470.35	36.95	716.68	82.39	52.4	123.0
New Hampshire	703.21	78.97	1,095.27	213.30	55.8	170.1
Vermont	629.80	31.00	959.80	99.34	52.4	220.5
Massachusetts	861.67	172.04	1,259.99	356.41	46.2	107.2
Rhode Island	712.43	120.33	965.96	247.83	35.6	106.0
Connecticut	870.02	92.03	1,230.61	230.90	41.4	150.9
MIDDLE ATLANTIC	$ 759.75	$ 91.43	$1,159.63	$ 268.22	52.6%	193.4%
New York	1,085.79	83.76	1,714.60	229.77	57.9	174.3
New Jersey	540.82	125.14	714.37	378.46	32.1	202.4
Pennsylvania	400.02	86.75	584.36	266.50	46.1	207.2
EAST NORTH CENTRAL	$ 339.76	$135.75	$ 437.58	$ 403.16	28.8%	197.0%
Ohio	361.13	233.33	421.22	543.04	16.6	132.7
Indiana	236.12	117.90	307.81	312.57	30.4	165.1
Illinois	357.79	132.29	481.97	502.93	34.7	280.2
Michigan	331.23	52.99	460.81	186.95	39.1	252.8
Wisconsin	361.66	92.76	468.17	344.83	29.5	271.7
WEST NORTH CENTRAL	$ 199.57	$ 77.57	$ 328.94	$ 283.72	64.8%	265.8%
Minnesota	350.85	113.41	512.06	355.25	50.2	213.2
Iowa	200.72	62.82	332.74	214.35	65.8	241.2
Missouri	178.40	69.21	297.87	321.42	67.0	364.4
North Dakota	256.91	64.19	362.49	233.05	41.1	263.1
South Dakota	137.41	17.96	326.30	92.30	137.5	413.9
Nebraska	105.26	78.98	140.98	240.40	33.9	204.4
Kansas	89.02	82.92	213.13	292.39	139.4	252.6
SOUTH ATLANTIC	$ 154.70	$ 85.10	$ 233.22	$ 303.23	50.8%	256.3%
Delaware	561.44	58.83	626.41	91.15	11.6	54.9
Maryland	349.87	135.45	402.13	395.42	14.9	191.9
Dist. of Columbia	252.59	434.27	407.86	1,140.63	61.5	162.7
Virginia	190.78	40.66	286.86	132.05	50.4	224.8
West Virginia	127.32	25.56	207.14	83.99	62.7	228.6
North Carolina	97.15	70.18	204.57	237.64	110.6	238.6
South Carolina	41.54	55.20	69.69	209.43	67.8	279.4
Georgia	92.01	61.68	178.10	223.01	93.6	261.6
Florida	131.35	114.57	242.28	525.71	84.5	358.9
SOUTH CENTRAL	$ 86.71	$ 47.22	$ 198.48	$ 186.55	128.9%	295.1%
Kentucky	77.13	74.29	146.67	231.41	90.2	211.5
Tennessee	139.69	41.53	276.07	162.67	97.6	291.7
Alabama	84.11	20.03	175.24	114.33	108.3	470.8
Mississippi	61.06	20.52	141.45	106.88	131.7	420.9
Arkansas	52.23	29.53	158.37	136.43	203.2	362.0
Louisiana	105.31	75.23	200.01	235.30	89.9	212.8
Oklahoma	58.81	80.24	203.01	253.62	245.2	216.1
Texas	86.18	42.72	213.63	200.09	147.9	368.4

(Continued)

40

Competition and Growth   41

Table 4-4 (Continued)

| State | Per Capita Savings | | | | Percentage Gain | |
| | 1950 | | 1959 | | | |
	Banks*	Assns.	Banks*	Assns.	Banks	Assns.
MOUNTAIN	$ 169.62	$ 64.60	$ 314.77	$ 242.29	85.6%	275.0%
Montana	165.24	48.71	343.16	156.40	107.7	221.1
Idaho	178.19	57.35	347.13	209.29	94.8	264.9
Wyoming	157.30	62.68	358.36	197.43	127.8	215.0
Colorado	169.37	88.44	312.12	373.46	84.3	322.3
New Mexico	68.78	43.52	164.51	159.04	139.2	265.4
Arizona	132.51	37.45	270.27	159.62	104.0	326.2
Utah	261.62	97.27	398.83	301.00	52.4	209.4
Nevada	385.53	32.29	538.15	235.32	39.6	628.8
PACIFIC	$ 478.83	$103.56	$ 594.21	$ 437.04	24.1%	322.0%
Alaska	194.74	9.48	245.53	56.30	26.1	493.9
Washington	305.59	111.79	723.39	351.72	136.7	214.6
Oregon	262.20	71.55	463.91	187.55	76.9	162.1
California	556.82	110.18	653.77	472.31	17.4	328.7
Hawaii	384.14	45.87	327.36	153.09	-14.8	233.7
UNITED STATES	$ 371.21	$ 91.38	$ 551.60	$ 308.08	48.6%	237.1%

*Time deposits of individuals, partnerships, and corporations.

Sources: Annual Reports, Comptroller of the Currency, 1950, 1959; Annual Statistical Reports, United States Savings and Loan League; Population, United States Bureau of the Census.

1947. Commercial bank savings just held their own, accounting for 31 percent of over-the-counter savings throughout the period. Mutual savings banks did somewhat better, but their performance was well below that of the other mutual-type institutions—savings and loan associations and credit unions. Government accounts (savings bonds and postal savings) fared most poorly.

Competition with Banks

Table 4-4 presents the per capita savings of individuals at banks and at savings associations as of December 31, 1950, along with comparable figures for 1959. In only one state—Delaware—did per capita savings at associations increase less than 100 percent, and the national average gain was 237 percent. At banks, the national average gain was a more modest 48.6 percent and, in all states except Oklahoma, per capita savings at banks grew more slowly than per capita savings at savings and loan associations. Relative to commercial bank savings, savings associations have reported their greatest inroads in the East North Central and the Pacific states. In both areas, savings gains at associations were six times more rapid than at banks. In general, the gains at associations become more pronounced as one moves across the nation from the east to the south and west.

Why are savings associations able to compete so successfully with banks for savings funds? The answer to this question is complex. There continues to be more that is not known than is known about why people save and why they save where they do. Some tentative judgments, however, are possible. Among the factors bearing on the question are these: return paid to savers by various institutions, geographic location and concentration of institutions, types of individuals holding accounts, and differences in merchandising techniques.

TABLE 4-5
Average Annual Yield on Selected Investments
1945-1960

Year	Savings and Loan Accounts	Savings Deposits in Comm'l Banks	Savings Deposits in Mutual Savings Banks	United States Bonds	Municipal High Grade Bonds	Corp. (AAA) Bonds
1945	2.5%	0.8%	1.7%	2.4%	1.7%	2.5%
1946	2.4	0.8	1.7	2.2	1.6	2.4
1947	2.3	0.9	1.7	2.3	2.3	2.9
1948	2.3	0.9	1.8	2.4	2.3	2.8
1949	2.3	0.9	1.9	2.3	2.1	2.6
1950	2.5	0.9	2.0	2.3	2.0	2.6
1951	2.6	1.1	2.1	2.6	2.0	2.9
1952	2.7	1.1	2.4	2.7	2.2	2.9
1953	2.8	1.1	2.5	2.9	2.8	3.2
1954	2.9	1.3	2.6	2.5	2.4	2.9
1955	2.9	1.4	2.7	2.8	2.6	3.1
1956	3.0	1.6	2.9	3.1	2.9	3.4
1957	3.3	2.1	3.0	3.5	3.6	3.9
1958	3.5	2.3	3.1	3.4	3.4	3.8
1959	3.7	2.5	3.2	4.1	3.7	4.4
1960	3.7	2.5	3.6	4.0	3.7	4.4

Source: Savings and loan association: effective rate of dividends, i.e., dividends distributed relative to average savings capital, based on data of members of Federal Home Loan Bank System; commercial banks: effective interest rate, based on data of Federal Reserve Board and Federal Deposit Insurance Corporation; mutual savings banks: "per deposit" rates reported by Association of Mutual Savings Banks; bond yields: Federal Reserve Board.

Return Paid to Savers. The return paid to savers by savings and loan associations is higher than the return securable from other deposit-type savings institutions. Table 4-5 shows the average annual yield on savings at savings and loan associations and on investments elsewhere between 1945 and 1960. The yield data were determined by dividing the total amount of money paid out to savers in interest and/or dividends at the respective institutions by the annual average of their savings account holdings. Because some individuals remove funds from institutions between dividend paying dates, the average yield on savings calculated in this way is lower than the return paid to savers who do receive dividends or interest. The assumption is made that withdrawals between dividend and interest computation dates are consistent from one institution to another. Regardless of statistical adjustments, savings and loan associa-

TABLE 4-6
Average Annual Yield on Savings and Increase in Savings
1947-1960

	Commercial Banks					Savings and Loan Associations				
Year	Average Yield[1]	Increase in Yield	Total Savings[2] (Billions of Dollars)	Savings Increase (Dollars)	Percent Increase	Average Yield[3]	Increase in Yield	Total Savings (Billions of Dollars)	Savings Increase (Dollars)	Percent Increase
1947	0.9%		$34.7			2.3%		$ 9.8		
1948	0.9	0.0	35.0	$0.3	0.9%	2.3	0.0	11.0	$1.2	12.2%
1949	0.9	0.0	35.1	0.1	2.9	2.3	0.0	12.5	1.5	13.6
1950	0.9	0.0	35.2	0.1	2.8	2.5	0.2	14.0	1.5	12.0
1951	1.1	0.2	36.6	1.4	4.0	2.6	0.1	16.1	2.1	15.0
1952	1.1	0.0	39.3	2.7	7.4	2.7	0.1	19.2	3.1	19.3
1953	1.1	0.0	42.0	2.7	6.9	2.8	0.1	22.8	3.6	18.8
1954	1.3	0.2	44.7	2.7	6.4	2.9	0.1	27.3	4.5	19.7
1955	1.4	0.1	46.3	1.6	3.6	2.9	0.0	32.2	4.9	17.9
1956	1.6	0.2	48.5	2.2	4.8	3.0	0.1	37.1	4.9	15.2
1957	2.1	0.5	53.7	5.2	10.7	3.3	0.2	41.9	4.8	12.9
1958	2.3	0.2	59.6	5.9	11.0	3.5	0.2	48.0	6.1	14.6
1959	2.5	0.2	62.7	3.1	5.2	3.75	0.25	54.5	6.5	13.5

[1]Effective interest rate, i.e., interest paid relative to average time deposits of individuals, partnerships, and corporations.
[2]Time deposits of individuals, partnerships, and corporations.
[3]Effective rate of dividends, i.e., dividends distributed relative to average savings capital.

Sources: Based on data of the Federal Deposit Insurance Corporation, Federal Reserve Board, and Federal Home Loan Bank Board.

43

tions do offer a more favorable yield than do mutual savings or commercial banks.

Increases in rates of return serve to stimulate savings flows into commercial banks. In Table 4-6, an attempt has been made to relate the
average return paid on savings accounts at associations and commercial
banks to the growth of savings at these institutions. The pattern is quite
consistent at banks. The increases in savings in 1951 and 1952, and again
in 1957 and 1958, accompanied upward shifts in the return to savers. The
analysis also indicates that it takes two years for the effects of rate changes
to subside. At savings and loan associations, no such pattern emerges.
Dividend rate increases occurred steadily throughout the period, as did
the gain in savings. Associations in 1960 offered savers, on the average,
1.2 percent more in earnings than the commercial banks and 0.3 percent
more than the mutual savings banks. Since 1950 the difference between
the rate paid to savers by commercial banks and by savings and loan
associations has narrowed. In that year the banks paid savers an average
yield of 0.9 percent, while savings associations paid 2.5 percent, a spread
of 1.6 percent. In 1959, the spread was 1.2 percent.

As more and more individuals accept it as fact that a 1 percent differential more than compensates them for any alleged difference in the
convenience or other assumed advantages of a bank savings account
over an association account, they may well switch funds from one institution to the other. There is reason to believe that once savers become
convinced that "you can get your money when you want it" at a savings
association, they tend to place their liquid savings in such institutions.
This hypothesis is supported by what happened during 1958 when
recessionary forces caused some associations to reduce rates. In a number of communities, both banks and associations suddenly found themselves offering an identical 3 percent return to savers. As expected, the
associations which reduced their rates to 3 percent experienced withdrawals. But when the funds withdrawn from associations were traced
by analyses of cancelled checks used in payment of withdrawals, it was
found that funds moved, not from associations to banks, but from associations in the community in question to associations in other communities
where the prevailing rate was in excess of 3 percent.

The difference in the rate of return can be termed with justification
the primary reason that savings association growth in savings volume
exceeds that at other deposit-type institutions. Rate of return, however,
is not the sole reason for the relatively better competitive performance
of associations on the savings side of their business.

Geographic Concentration. Over one-half of the combined savings
deposits at commercial banks and mutual savings banks can be found in
the northeastern part of the United States, that is, New England and the
New York–New Jersey–Pennsylvania area. Capital formation in this sec-

tion of the country attained a level sufficient to support massive financial institutions much earlier than in other parts of the country. Furthermore, the sophistication of individuals regarding money matters generally is higher in eastern money centers. As evidence, consider the fact that this area was most severely affected by the shifting of funds from financial institutions into U.S. Treasury obligations during late 1959 and early 1960. The Treasury reports that approximately 54 percent of the "Magic Fives" of October 1959 which were allocated to individuals were sold in the New York and Boston Federal Reserve Districts (Table 4-7).

TABLE 4-7
Distribution by Federal Reserve Districts of Portion of "Magic Fives"
Allocated to Individuals
1959

District	Percentage of Total	District	Percentage of Total
Boston	6.6%	St. Louis	4.3%
New York	47.4	Minneapolis	1.7
Philadelphia	5.1	Kansas City	3.5
Cleveland	4.6	Dallas	2.8
Richmond	4.0	San Francisco	5.0
Atlanta	3.7	Treasury	0.4
Chicago	10.9	Total	100.0%

Source: United States Treasury Department.

In the savings and loan business the concentration of savings is not nearly so great. Only 22 percent of savings and loan assets can be found in the northeastern part of the United States. In sections of the country outside the East, associations are more often than not the dominant savings institution. The growth of associations has been most marked in areas where the demands for home building funds have been strongest and where the earning power of associations on mortgages has been strongest. In a sense, rapid growth and a strong real estate market have been both the cause and the effect of savings and loan development.

Promotional Efforts. Savings associations are aggressive and enthusiastic promoters of savings and thrift, spending approximately 2.7 percent of their gross income on advertising and promotion. Promotion efforts during the past decade have been largely on the savings side and have included national advertising through the Savings and Loan Foundation. The relative amount of savings and loan dollars going into advertising between 1950 and 1960 averaged 0.13 percent of year-end assets—a larger percentage than was employed by any other major financial institution. As mentioned, these funds were spent primarily for one specific purpose —to promote savings. Promotional efforts take the form of contests, premiums, and gifts for new accounts as well as advertising.

Commercial banks spend more dollars for advertising than associations do, but they distribute their promotional funds over many more departments. Among the activities advertised other than savings are regular checking accounts, automobile loans, personal loans, bank-by-mail, farm production loans, repair loans, and safe-deposit facilities. •

Characteristics of Savers and Borrowers. Part of the explanation for the relatively better performance of savings and loan associations as

TABLE 4-8
Comparison of Characteristics of Savers
At Savings and Loan Associations with Total Population
Percentage Distribution[1]

	U.S. Population	Four Far West Assns.	Eight Midwest Assns.	One Southeast Assn.	One Southwest Assn.
Number of questionnaries mailed:		2,309	4,743	8,000	44,000
Number returned		805	1,863	1,800	9,200
Percentage response		37.0%	39.0%	22.5%	20.9%
1. Occupation (head of family):					
Professional or executive ⎱	21.7%	26.0%	27.6%	31.2%	21.9%
Merchant or self-employed ⎰		8.8	7.1	8.1	8.0
Skilled or semi-skilled	36.5	14.5	17.2	10.2	17.2
Clerical or sales	20.9	6.5	11.1	14.1	16.0
Student	--	1.8	7.6	11.4	5.9
Retired	--	29.7	14.1	12.0	13.3
Other	20.9	12.7	12.5	13.0	17.6
2. Family income - 1958					
Under $1,000	5.6	4.7	--	5.9	8.1
$1,000 - $3,999	29.7	22.7	23.0	18.9	25.6
$4,000 - $4,999	13.4	11.2	11.3	10.7	19.2
$5,000 - $9,999	41.3	42.4	38.6	40.1	33.7
$10,000 and up	10.0	19.0	20.7	24.4	13.5
3. Education					
Grammar school, 1-8 years	48.3	14.6	19.2	17.3	17.7
Some high school	17.4	18.2	15.4	14.1	16.5
High school graduate	20.7	15.8	20.6	12.3	23.8
Some college	7.4	26.5	17.5	21.7	21.4
College graduate	6.2	24.9	23.4	34.5	16.9
4. Age					
1 - 18 years ⎱	44.1	0.8	9.8	18.2	6.5
19 - 24 years ⎰		1.8	4.4	5.1	7.2
25 - 34 years	13.4	10.6	10.5	11.6	17.2
35 - 44 years	13.5	17.2	18.3	16.7	21.7
45 - 54 years	11.5	20.4	18.0	17.5	17.6
55 - 64 years	8.7	18.1	17.8	16.5	14.6
65 years and over	8.8	31.1	20.9	14.4	15.3

[1]Percentage breakdowns are based on the total number of replies to each question.

Source: Population Characteristics—Department of Commerce. Occupation, family income and age—1958; education—1950. Saver characteristics—United States League.

compared with other financial institutions in the solicitation of savings may lie in the characteristics of the customers attracted to the various institutions. Some data are available on the characteristics of savers at savings and loan associations. They were obtained through mail surveys of savings and loan customers conducted in Albert Lea, Minnesota; Aurora, Illinois; Baton Rouge, Louisiana; Dayton, Ohio; San Antonio, Texas; and San Diego, California. Table 4-8 shows the characteristics of these savers in several of the cities. The variations from city to city were surprisingly slight. In each instance, savings and loan savers were relatively high on the educational ladder as well as in income. These data, though sketchy, are submitted to stimulate further and more thoroughgoing research into savers and savings habits. Unfortunately, no comparable data are available on the characteristics of savers at commercial banks or mutual savings banks.

On the mortgage side, families who use the conventional home loan to buy their homes seem to represent a cross section of American families. The typical single-family conventional loan borrower is approximately thirty-seven years of age, has a median annual income of $7,300, has purchased a six-room house for $17,100, and received a mortgage of $11,100 to help him purchase his home. He has made a down payment of approximately $6,000 in cash or equivalent, a ratio of 32 percent of the purchase price of the home. These facts were the result of a survey of almost 7,000 home mortgages made by savings and loan associations in major metropolitan centers during 1957. The characteristics of buyers of new homes and existing homes are shown in Table 4-9.

TABLE 4-9
**Characteristics of Single-Family Home Buyers Using Conventional Loans
in Twenty-Two Metropolitan Areas, 1957**

	All Homes	New Homes	Existing Homes
Median age of borrower	37 years	36 years	39 years
Median annual income of borrower	$ 7,300	$ 7,625	$ 6,950
Number of rooms in house	6	--	--
Median purchase price of house	$17,100	$18,600	$15,600
Median loan characteristics:			
Amount of mortgage	$11,100	$11,600	$11,100
Down payment (percentage of purchase price)	32.7%	31.2%	35.1%
Loan-to-purchase price ratio	67.3%	68.8%	64.9%

Source: United States Savings and Loan League Survey of Borrower Characteristics, 1958.

The home buyer purchasing a new home tended to be slightly younger than an individual who purchased an existing property, and he paid more for his house than did the existing home buyer. The individual purchasing a single-family house through a savings and loan association

TABLE 4-10
Home Mortgage Recordings,[1]
By Type of Lender
1940–1960
(Dollar Amounts in Millions)

Year	Savings and Loan Associations	Insurance Companies	Commercial Banks	Mutual Savings Banks	Individuals and Others	Total, All Lenders Number	Volume
1940	$ 1,283	$ 334	$1,006	$ 170	$ 1,238	1,456,000	$ 4,031
1946	3,483	503	2,712	548	3,343	2,497,000	10,589
1947	3,650	847	3,004	597	3,631	2,567,000	11,729
1948	3,629	1,016	2,664	745	3,828	2,535,000	11,882
1949	3,646	1,046	2,446	750	3,940	2,488,000	11,828
1950	5,060	1,618	3,365	1,064	5,072	3,032,000	16,179
1951	5,295	1,615	3,370	1,013	5,112	2,878,000	16,405
1952	6,452	1,420	3,600	1,137	5,409	3,028,000	18,018
1953	7,365	1,480	3,680	1,327	5,895	3,164,000	19,747
1954	8,312	1,768	4,239	1,501	7,154	3,458,000	22,974
1955	10,452	1,932	5,616	1,858	8,626	3,913,000	28,484
1956	9,532	1,799	5,458	1,824	8,475	3,602,000	27,088
1957	9,217	1,472	4,264	1,430	7,861	3,246,000	24,244
1958	10,516	1,460	5,204	1,640	8,568	3,441,000	27,388
1959	13,094	1,523	5,832	1,780	10,006	3,782,000	32,235
1960	12,158	1,318	4,520	1,557	9,788	3,472,477	29,341

Percentage Distribution

Year	Savings and Loan Associations	Insurance Companies	Commercial Banks	Mutual Savings Banks	Individuals and Others	Total, All Lenders
1940	31.8%	8.3%	25.0%	4.2%	30.7%	100.0%
1946	32.9	4.8	25.6	5.2	31.5	100.0
1947	31.1	7.2	25.6	5.1	31.0	100.0
1948	30.5	8.6	22.4	6.3	32.2	100.0
1949	30.9	8.8	20.7	6.3	33.3	100.0
1950	31.3	10.0	20.8	6.6	31.3	100.0
1951	32.3	9.8	20.5	6.2	31.2	100.0
1952	35.8	7.9	20.0	6.3	30.0	100.0
1953	37.4	7.5	18.6	6.7	29.8	100.0
1954	36.2	7.7	18.5	6.5	31.1	100.0
1955	36.7	6.8	19.7	6.5	30.3	100.0
1956	35.2	6.6	20.2	6.7	31.3	100.0
1957	38.0	6.1	17.6	5.9	32.4	100.0
1958	38.4	5.3	19.0	6.0	31.3	100.0
1959	40.6	4.7	18.1	5.5	31.1	100.0
1960	41.4	4.5	15.4	5.3	33.4	100.0

[1]Non-farm mortgage recordings of $20,000 or less.

Source: Federal Home Loan Bank Board.

was probably purchasing his second or third home. Other League studies indicate the average age of first-time home buyers at savings and loan associations actually is closer to thirty rather than thirty-seven, as reported for all borrowers in the 1957 investigation. A comparison of the characteristics of conventional borrowers as revealed by this study, with data published in the reports of the Federal Housing Administration regarding borrowers using its mortgage plan, indicate conventional financing is more extensively available to lower income borrowers and to lower priced houses than is the financing sponsored by government agencies. The breadth of coverage of the conventional financing is especially significant in view of the slow but steady rise since the end of World War II in the median income of FHA borrowers and the median initial amount of the insured mortgage, both of which appear to have risen more than can be accounted for by increases in income or construction costs during the period.

Competition for Loans and Investments. As lenders, savings and loan associations compete with other lenders almost exclusively in a single field—the home mortgage market. The most adequate measure of competition in home mortgage financing can be found in the statistical series known as *mortgages recorded* compiled by the Federal Home Loan Bank Board. These statistics cover both number and dollar amount of recordings for some six types of mortgages, and cover loans of $20,000 or less, usually to finance one- to four-family houses.

Table 4-10 shows home mortgage recordings by type of lender in millions of dollars and by percentage distribution from 1940 through 1960.

Savings associations lead all other types of lenders in the field of home mortgage financing. Their recordings in 1959 amounted to $13.1 billion, a new peak. For the first time, they recorded 40 percent of the nation's home mortgages, a modern high for any type of lender. Since 1950, there has been only one year (1956) in which associations did not register a gain in their relative position. Thus, associations have not only handled the steadily growing volume of mortgage financing which has accompanied nationwide growing aggregate real estate activity, but at the same time have made competitive inroads on other lenders.

Among other lenders, commercial banks in 1959 recorded about 18 percent of home mortgage volume. "Other mortgage lenders," principally mortgage bankers who resell loans to insurance companies and banks, made approximately 19 percent of all loans. Individuals as lenders were responsible for 12 percent of aggregate recordings. Insurance companies and mutual savings banks each directly recorded approximately 5 percent of total volume, according to Federal Home Loan Bank data.

Mortgage recordings data, however, do not provide a completely accurate picture of home mortgage financing. For one thing, they include only mortgage loans of $20,000 or less, and thus understate the total volume of home financing. This deficiency, however, tends to be balanced somewhat by the inclusion in the data of certain loans on properties other than residences. Furthermore, mortgage recordings as reported measure principally loan originations and do not reflect the holdings of certain institutions—notably insurance companies—which purchase mortgages in considerable volume.

The conventional home loan continues to be the mainstay of the home mortgage market. This is true despite an occasional upsurge in government-underwritten mortgages (FHA and VA loans). In 1960, conventional mortgages accounted for $22.8 billion, or 78 percent, of the year's $29.3 billion in recordings. Table 4-11 shows lending figures for 1960 by conventional, FHA, and VA recordings on a dollar as well as on a percentage basis.

TABLE 4-11
Home Mortgage Recordings,[1]
by Type of Lender and Type of Loan, 1960
(In Millions of Dollars)

	Conventional	FHA	VA	Total
Savings and loan associations	$11,078	$ 658	$ 422	$12,158
Commercial banks	3,343	1,035	142	4,520
Insurance companies	1,072	198	48	1,318
Mutual savings banks	1,047	253	257	1,557
Mortgage companies	2,388	2,301	1,098	5,787
Others	3,827	156	18	4,001
All lenders	$22,755	$4,601	$1,985	$29,341

Percentage Distribution

	Conventional	FHA	VA	Total
Savings and loan associations	91.1%	5.4%	3.5%	100.0%
Commercial banks	74.0	22.9	3.1	100.0
Insurance companies	81.3	15.1	3.6	100.0
Mutual savings banks	67.2	16.3	16.5	100.0
Mortgage companies	41.3	39.7	19.0	100.0
Others	95.7	3.9	0.4	100.0
All lenders	77.6%	15.6%	6.8%	100.0%

[1]Mortgage recordings of $20,000 or less, reported by Federal Home Loan Bank Board.

Source: Federal Housing Administration, Veterans Administration, U.S. Savings and Loan League.

Competition between savings associations and other mortgage lenders is considerably more intense in some cities and areas than others. Generally, it is most noticeable in those areas where associations have less than 50 percent of the home mortgage market. In most respects, the observations made earlier in this monograph about competition among savings and loan associations apply equally well to competition between associations and other types of lenders.

Data on home mortgage holdings rather than recordings is as follows: Savings associations, at the end of 1959, had 78 percent of their aggregate assets in mortgages on one- to four-family homes. At mutual savings banks, such mortgages comprised 43 percent of assets; insurance companies reported 21 percent of their assets in home mortgages; and commercial banks held only 8 percent of their assets in mortgages.

The competitive strength of savings and loan associations on the lending side, then, stems from their position as the specialty shops of home finance, their essentially local character requiring intensive cultivation of immediate markets, and the strong demand for their product, that is, mortgage financing. In periods of rapidly rising population and income, when strong demands for new and upgraded shelter exist, institutions holding themselves out as primary financiers of such needs find rapid growth essential to the performance of the mission assigned to them in our economy. If existing institutions do not measure up to their assignments, society more often than not finds other means and new institutions through which to get the job done.

The level of home building and real estate activity has a vital influence on the development of savings and loan associations. Associations can grow only if they are able to put savings to work at a profitable return. Opportunities for mortgage lending usually must be available within the lending area of the individual institutions. In general, the greater the opportunities for mortgage lending, the greater the growth of the savings and loan business. Since the bulk of the home building and real estate activity in this country during the 1950's took place in urban areas, savings and loan development also turned out to be largely urban in character. Seven out of every ten housing starts during that decade took place in a metropolitan area, a county, or contiguous counties containing at least one city of 50,000 or more inhabitants.[2]

Expanding the Savings and Loan Business

Lending

Associations could develop additional lending business by offering a lower rate for mortgage loans than competitors are offering. Such a practice, however, is not usual. More often than not, associations will quote lending rates at, or even slightly above, competitive levels, competing for loans with each other and with other lenders on a nonprice or service basis. A higher-than-market rate is possible because associations can offer a number of services to buyers and sellers of real estate which other lenders cannot match. As local lenders, operating in a geographically limited market, associations specialize in providing very rapid service on real estate transactions, closing loans in a matter of days. In addition, they can readily tailor loans to meet local demands and the specifications of the property because they understand the local laws and codes. They

---

[2] For detailed data, see *Housing Statistics*, Housing and Home Finance Agency.

also provide more complete home financing service: a single institution can offer the commitment to a builder, a construction loan, and a take-out or permanent home loan. Few, if any, other lenders do the entire job. Associations are authorized to make mortgage loans for as high as 80 percent of the appraised value of the property, for maturities up to twenty-five years; in some instances, they can lend up to 90 percent of the appraised value. (Banks and insurance companies have a legal maximum loan-to-value ratio of three-fourths of appraised value and a twenty-year maturity in most states.) Of importance to builders and real estate brokers, associations generally are in the local mortgage market on a continuous basis and strive to honor requests for financing from builders or developers at all times.

One reason savings and loan associations can offer borrowers more extended terms on mortgage contracts stems from the nature of the savings accounts they hold. The accounts at thrift institutions seldom exhibit a high velocity of turnover. The time elapsing between the dates of deposit and withdrawal at savings associations averaged between three and one-half and four years during the ten years from 1949 to 1958. Although the average life of a savings and loan account now is much shorter than the six years and eight months reported for 1940, it is still lengthy by institutional standards. Savings accounts at mutual savings banks have been turning over in slightly under four years. Time deposits and savings accounts of commercial banks turn over about once in two years. By way of contrast, the velocity of demand deposits at commercial banks in six large cities, excluding New York, was approximately thirty times a year.[3]

The relative permanence of savings accounts in savings associations makes it possible for these institutions to invest a large percentage of their funds in long-term mortgages on residential property. It also permits safety of operation without the maintenance of a large liquid reserve. Both of these factors enhance the over-all earning capacity of the association, in that a larger percentage of total assets may be invested, and yields on long-term mortgages tend to be higher than those on short-term obligations.

The Federal Home Loan Bank System is another important source of association liquidity. When an association does face a need for liquid funds to meet sudden withdrawals or payments, it can call on its regional Federal Home Loan Bank to provide such funds. Borrowings as high as 12 percent of savings capital are permitted. Funds may be advanced to

---

[3] The data on velocity of savings accounts are computed on the basis of the ratio of withdrawals to average total savings. For mutual savings banks, an average of three dates per year was used; Federal Reserve Member Bank quarterly data underlie commercial bank figures; the savings and loan figures are based on an average of beginning and ending dates for each year.

smooth out imbalances developing between savings inflow and loan demand seasonally and over the housing cycle, as well as for the payment of unusual withdrawals.

Savings

Associations seem to rely heavily on price to expand their savings business. The price offered to savers for their funds has been rising steadily at associations since 1949. In that year, associations were returning to savers an average of 2.3 percent on their savings accounts. By 1959 the yield to savers had been lifted to 3.75 percent. As has been mentioned, savings has also been promoted from time to time through the use of limited gifts and premiums.

Savings and loan managers are constantly seeking new ways to tap additional pools of savings funds. They support actively the efforts of the National Thrift Committee and its promotion of thrift among American families, school children, and other groups. The development of thrift habits among consumers is encouraged because it can produce at a fair cost sizable amounts of funds needed to meet the ever-increasing demands from the home mortgage market of this country.

Growth Prospects for the Business

The savings and loan business is optimistic about its growth prospects. Savings and loan managers expect an average growth of more than 10 percent per year over the next five years. These estimates are based on a survey of 1,700 associations conducted during the spring of 1960 by the Research Department of the United States League.

In a more thoroughgoing and detailed projection of what the next decade may hold for the savings and loan business, a research team of the Indiana University School of Business arrived at similar estimates.[4] The principal findings of the Indiana research are these: During the 1960's an average of 1.3 to 1.4 million new housing units will be started annually. Total expenditures for new dwelling units and for alterations and additions to existing housing will come to $247 billion, compared with $163 billion for the previous decade. The total population is expected to grow by 33 million persons. The number of persons employed will increase 13.5 million, and output per employed person will rise approximately 25 percent. The gross national product will go from approximately $500 billion in 1960 to $750 billion in 1970. Income per house-

---

[4] The results of this research appear in a booklet entitled "The Next Decade . . . and Its Opportunities for the Savings and Loan Business," a preliminary report prepared for the United States Savings and Loan League by the School of Business, Indiana University, Bloomington, Indiana, November 1, 1959.

TABLE 4-12
An Estimate of New Housing Starts in the Decade of the Sixties

Increase in non-farm households 10,100,000
Add: Housing units lost through destruction,
conversion to other use, merger, etc. 3,500,000
Increase in vacancies 400,000
Seasonal and other "second home" requirements 750,000
Gross need for new housing units 14,750,000
Less: Units supplied by conversion, trailers, public housing, etc. 1,250,000
New private non-farm housing starts 13,500,000
Annual average 1,350,000

Source: "The Next Decade . . . and Its Opportunities for the Savings and Loan Business,"
School of Business, Indiana University, November 1, 1959.

hold and the proportion of family spending going into housing will also increase.

As a consequence of these expectations, savings associations will continue to grow at a rapid rate during the 1960's, passing the $100 billion mark in total assets before the end of 1965 and reaching $165 billion by 1970. Despite such substantial growth, associations will not dominate the home mortgage lending markets because the volume of mortgage lending is expected to increase at a similar rate. In 1970, associations will still hold less than half of the total outstanding residential mortgage debt.

The Indiana research group recognized fully the hazards of making specific numerical projections or estimates. Yet they arrived at definite estimates, so that, for the time being, savings association executives would have as sound a basis for long-range planning as possible. To the extent that the assumptions prove to be inaccurate, appropriate revisions can be made in long-range plans.

Population and Housing

It appears almost certain that there will be more than 200 million persons in the United States by 1970. Using Census Bureau projections, the Indiana study concludes that an additional 33 million persons will require housing in the decade ahead. Looking more deeply into the growth in population, there will be a significant increase in the number of households, but an equally significant decrease in the number of people between the ages of thirty and forty. Because of this carry-over of the low birth rate in the 1930's, relatively fewer persons will be in the working population, and larger numbers will be found among the very young and very old. From the point of view of the savings and loan business, these internal shifts will affect savings more adversely than lending.

The Indiana study indicates that the percentage of total spending that goes into housing is relatively constant at all income levels. Thus, as personal income rises during the next decade, more dollars will be spent on shelter.

Against this background of estimated population, income, household formation, and housing expenditures, the Indiana study moves into the critical business of projecting housing starts and mortgage lending. New private non-farm housing starts are expected to total between 13 million and 14 million units during the decade, an average of approximately 1.35 million starts per year (Table 4-12). This level of activity is not very much greater than the estimated 12 million dwelling units started during the 1950's.

As consumers demand larger units and higher quality housing, the number of dollars allocated to residential construction will rise more sharply than the number of starts. Considering this factor and assuming constant prices, the average annual construction bill will rise from $16.3 billion during the 1950's to $24.7 billion in the decade ahead.

Residential mortgage debt outstanding is expected to continue moving upward from $53.6 billion in 1950 and $145.3 billion in 1959 to over $200 billion in 1964 and $300 billion by 1970 (Table 4-13).

Attracting Savings Capital

Savings and loan associations finance home ownership almost exclusively. The Indiana appraisal of the future market for associations suggests that the demand for home financing services will be strong during the coming decade. New homes must be constructed to shelter an increasing number of households; to permit the continued migration of families from farm to city, from city to suburb, from North to East to South and West; to replace housing unfit for use or destroyed; to provide second homes for families who wish and can afford them; to enable American families to improve the quality of their housing as standards of living continue to rise.

The big "if" in the adequate service of this market is the ability of associations to attract savings capital at a cost sufficiently low to make mortgage lending by associations competitive. Although the annual increases in total debt are building up a growing pool of repayment funds available for reinvestment, such funds will not be sufficient to do the job. Increases in the cost of the average house, the shortening of down payments and the lengthening of maturities, and the tendency for existing borrowers to refinance their loans to obtain cash as soon as equity has built up, intensify the need for associations to develop new savings.

In order to accomplish the home financing tasks which lie ahead, the Indiana research group feels that associations will have to learn how to tap pension funds and other large pools of accumulated savings. It also feels that associations will have to develop varied forms of savings instruments tailored to consumer needs, including one which will reward

56

Competition and Growth

TABLE 4-13
Residential Construction Expenditures and
Increase in Residential Mortgage Debt
1950–1970
(in Billions of Dollars)

Year	Residential Construction Expenditures[1]	Increase in Residential Mortgage Debt	Residential Mortgage Debt Outstanding
Actual (in current prices)			
1950	$ 14.1	$ 8.7	$ 53.6
1951	12.5	7.8	61.4
1952	12.8	7.5	68.9
1953	13.8	8.2	77.1
1954	15.4	10.2	87.3
1955	18.7	13.4	100.6
1956	17.7	11.4	112.1
1957	17.0	9.6	121.7
1958	17.9	12.3	134.0
Estimated (in 1958 prices)			
1959	$ 18.3	$ 11.3	$145.3
1960	19.1	11.9	157.2
1961	20.0	12.2	169.4
1962	21.0	13.0	182.4
1963	22.0	13.6	196.0
1964	22.9	14.2	210.2
1965	24.0	14.9	225.1
1966	25.0	15.5	240.6
1967	26.2	16.2	256.8
1968	27.4	17.0	273.8
1969	28.6	17.7	291.5
1970	29.9	18.5	310.0
1951-60:			
Total	$163.2	$103.6	--
Average	16.3	10.4	--
1961-70:			
Total	$247.0	$152.8	--
Average	24.7	15.3	--

[1]Includes additions and alterations, but excludes repair and maintenance.

Source: "The Next Decade . . . and Its Opportunities for the Savings and Loan Business," School of Business, Indiana University, November, 1, 1959.

adequately the investor who keeps his funds with associations for a long period of time and does not insist on being able to withdraw on demand.

Savings and loan managers, the University scholars advise, should assume that their business pays too much for money and has excessive operating expenses. Regardless of whether these assumptions are true, nothing will do more to assure continued growth than to believe that they are.

Competitive Environment

What happens to the savings and loan business will depend also on what competitors do, how they react to continued rapid growth of savings and loan associations (if that turns out to be the course of events), and how they react to estimates of their own future growth. While it is not inconceivable that competition for mortgages and mortgage funds may well result in the development of wholly new types of financial institutions or in the vigorous entry of pension funds into the mortgage field, a more reasonable assumption is that the present mortgage lending institutions—savings and loan associations, mutual savings banks, life insurance companies, and commercial banks—will continue to meet this need.

Table 4-14 estimates the relative share of residential mortgage debt that will be held by the major lending institutions and others in 1970. The share of total mortgages held by savings associations will rise at the expense of other holders. By 1970, mortgages outstanding are expected to reach 44 percent of the total residential mortgage debt. As residential mortgage lenders, associations will have moved farther out in front but

TABLE 4-14
Percentage of Total Residential Mortgage Debt Outstanding by Type of Lender
1950–1970

	1950	1960	1970
Savings and loan associations	25.0%	35.7%	44.4%
Life insurance companies	20.7	20.2	18.5
Mutual savings banks	13.2	13.7	11.2
Commercial banks	19.3	13.2	12.0
Individuals and others	21.8	17.2	13.9
Total	100.0%	100.0%	100.0%

Source: "The Next Decade . . . and Its Opportunities for the Savings and Loan Business," School of Business, Indiana University, November 1, 1959.

certainly will not have driven their competitors out of business. With over 80 percent of their assets in residential mortgages, and confined legally to this activity, associations are in the best position to meet the burgeoning demand for home mortgage funds during the decade ahead.

The declining relative importance of mutual savings banks in the world of finance results chiefly from their limited number and their concentration in the northeastern part of the United States. Although they acquire some mortgages from the rapidly growing areas of the South and West, they are not able to tap these areas effectively for savings funds.

Life insurance companies are expected to increase the proportion of residential mortgages in their portfolios very little during the next decade. These institutions will be faced with strong demands from business for funds to finance plant expansion. In addition, growth in total assets may be less vigorous, since lower premium forms of insurance are rising in popularity.

CHART 4-2

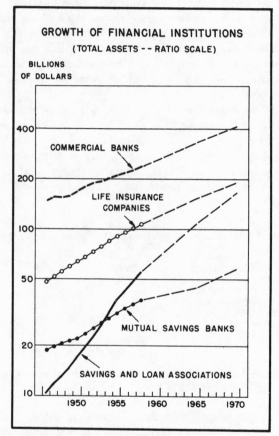

Source: Indiana University, "The Next Decade,"
United States Savings and Loan League.

Commercial banks have never allocated a very high percentage of their assets to residential mortgages, and it is difficult to predict what course they will take. Past experience, banking traditions, and laws and regulations indicate, however, that they are not likely to increase the ratio of mortgages to their total loans and investments.

Continued growth of the savings and loan business, bringing it to $165 billion in total assets by 1970, can be effected if the conditions outlined above are broadly met. In addition, the business will need vigorous support by its regulatory agencies and ambitious but continued careful management of existing savings and loan associations. Steady improvement of the products offered to the public, conventional mortgage loans, and savings instruments will be vital to future growth.

All financial institutions are expected to increase in asset size during this decade (Chart 4-2). Although the growth of savings and loan associations is expected to be at a greater rate than that of other institutions, by 1970 their total assets still will be less than those of insurance companies, and much less than those of commercial banks.

Chapter 5

ROLE IN THE
SAVINGS PROCESS

Liquidity

In its broadest sense, liquidity can be defined as the relative ability to transform one's assets into generally acceptable means of payment at particular points in time without delay. Individuals are said to have a preference or desire for liquidity for three principal reasons:

1) *Transaction motive.* A supply of money must be held in order to permit regular and continuous expenditures out of an income received only at specific intervals. The flow of funds must be equated.

2) *Precautionary motive.* A supply of money may be desired for emergency use—to tide one over in case of misfortune, such as illness, accident, or loss of employment. In this instance, ready cash is the first line of defense. Other assets may be converted into money, but the risk of loss in so doing may be great.

3) *Speculative motive.* Individuals sometimes hold pools of money temporarily while awaiting the passage of a time interval in which they hope their economic opportunities will improve. They hope to outguess the market, in a sense. If interest rates (in the broad definition) never changed, the speculative motive would not be an important one. But this is not the case. When considering savings associations, however, the first two reasons have the greatest relevance.

The rate of return on savings may be considered, not as a reward for savings, but rather as a payment for giving up liquidity. Other things being equal, people usually prefer to hold money rather than less liquid assets. Money is the ultimate in liquidity, even though its purchasing power may rise and fall. Any other assets into which a person may transform his dollars will have an uncertain money value determinable only when he converts the assets back into money. Interest is paid in part to persuade people to transfer their money into less liquid assets.

Consideration of liquidity, as it applies to financial institutions, presumes a certain hierarchy of assets by liquidity. It also presumes standardized criteria among the financial supervisory and regulatory agencies for the definition of liquidity in the legal sense.

Debates regarding what is or what is not appropriate liquidity are more pronounced in the savings and loan field today than anywhere else. Some observers, viewing what they hold to be the changed character of associations (or better, perhaps, changed liquidity attitudes of consumers toward these institutions), maintain that the liquidity criteria at associations must be made comparable to those of commercial banks. Others would refute the severity of such standards. Differences of opinion exist among the most thoughtful analysts of savings and loan matters, as well as among practitioners in the field. Criteria advocated vary according to the degree to which individual critics identify the savings association as a banking operation and attempt to judge its liquidity by the current tenets of commonly accepted banking policy.

The questions to be examined, then, are these: Do savings associations, in accepting funds from the public, perform a banking operation which requires specified minimums of liquidity? What factors tend to explain any appropriate differences in liquidity criteria for judging the various institutions? Considering the safety of savings funds of individuals, can a philosophy of liquidity be developed for savings associations more appropriate to it than that used by banks? To what degree must financial institutions prepare for the severest of potential strains on their system? How much reliance can be placed on an average performance by institutions in developing a liquidity concept?

Liquidity Defined

In its strictest sense, liquidity would consist only of cash on hand plus assets that can be converted into cash without delay and without loss, or with no greater loss than has been provided for through reserves. Cash and government bonds valued at market prices are the best examples of such assets. Under this definition, loans made by financial institutions— whether amortized or not, whether short- or long-term—must be excluded from liquidity. The possible exceptions would be few.

This concept of liquidity is the one generally accepted by commercial bankers and by the supervisory agencies regulating commercial banks and most other financial institutions. In the savings and loan business similar criteria are generally held.

Table 5-1 presents the trend in liquidity at savings associations under these standards. Since 1947 liquidity has declined from 23.6 percent of total savings to 11.7 percent. The greater part of the decline took place during the late 1940's, when mortgage loans became available in volume and government obligations could be liquidated without loss.

The effects on liquidity of the availability of investments in home loans

TABLE 5-1
Liquid Assets and Liquidity Ratio of Savings and Loan Associations
1947-1960

Year End	Liquid Assets[1] (Millions of Dollars)	Liquidity Ratio[2]
1947	$2,300	23.6%
1948	2,118	19.3
1949	2,342	18.8
1950	2,440	17.2
1951	2,688	16.6
1952	3,097	16.0
1953	3,423	14.9
1954	3,967	14.6
1955	4,404	13.7
1956	4,859	13.2
1957	5,317	12.7
1958	6,356	13.3
1959	6,660	12.2
1960 p	7,301	11.7

p — Preliminary.
[1]Total of cash on hand and in banks, plus U.S. Government securities.
[2]Liquid assets as a percentage of savings capital.

Source: United States Savings and Loan League, based on data of the Federal Home Loan Bank Board.

are quite apparent. As home building activity and the demand for mortgage funds rises, liquidity tends to decline. When home building and the corresponding requests for mortgages ease, as happened in 1958, institutions tend to build up their liquidity. This happens because inflows from repayments and new savings tend to be more stable than mortgage demand and to run ahead of the demand for new mortgage funds in times of ease.

Bank Liquidity and Association Liquidity Compared

Table 5-2 compares on the strictest terms the liquidity of savings associations with that of commercial banks and mutual savings banks. Liquidity ratios at both types of banking institutions are considerably higher than those at savings associations. During the postwar years a pronounced decline has occurred in the liquidity of mutual savings banks; liquidity ratios are one-third what they were in 1947. A more moderate decline has taken place in the liquidity ratio at commercial banks. Savings and loan associations reduced their ratio of cash and government bonds to savings earlier in the period than did other institutions. Recent reductions in liquidity have been relatively greater at banks as tight money pressures have pinched the supply of loanable funds.

Differences in liquid asset holdings stem from the very nature of the various institutions. A vehicle should be built for the load it is designed

TABLE 5-2
Liquidity Ratios of Selected Financial Institutions
1947-1960

Year	Savings Associations[1]	Commercial Banks[2]	Mutual Savings Banks[2]
1947	23.6%	74.0%	72.4%
1948	19.3	70.8	67.1
1949	18.8	70.7	63.8
1950	17.2	65.8	58.2
1951	16.6	64.3	51.2
1952	16.0	62.4	45.7
1953	14.9	61.2	41.8
1954	14.6	60.2	37.1
1955	13.7	56.3	33.4
1956	13.2	54.3	29.6
1957	12.7	52.9	26.6
1958	13.3	53.3	24.0
1959	12.2	49.3	22.0
1960	11.7	49.2	19.6

[1]Ratio of cash and U.S. Government bonds to savings capital.
[2]Ratio of cash and U.S. Government bonds to total deposits.

Source: Based on data of the Federal Deposit Insurance Corporation and the Federal Home Loan Bank Board.

to carry. Savings associations do not pretend to be designed to carry a commercial bank's load. According to Federal Reserve statistics, commercial banks outside New York City expect to honor checks in an amount equal to their total demand deposit liability on an average of every thirteen days. In the larger banks a complete weekly turnover of demand deposits would not be considered uncommon. By contrast, savings withdrawal experience at savings associations is of a much lower order. Withdrawals during 1960 averaged 2.4 percent of total savings per month as compared with 2.5 percent in 1959 and 2.1 percent in 1949. This is a key fact in liquidity considerations and presents a picture vastly different from what some observers have been led to believe.

Expressed another way, savings funds at savings associations turn over once every three years and seven months; at mutual savings banks the turnover rate is once every three years and ten months; at commercial banks time deposits are estimated to turn over once every two years; and demand deposits in banks outside New York City turn over approximately thirty times *each* year. To the extent that liquidity requirements are tied to turnover of funds in normal times, the differences in the liquid holdings of the various institutions may be explained.

The most serious withdrawal demands placed on savings associations during the postwar years occurred during the summer of 1950 when the Korean conflict struck and consumers went on a buying spree. This surge of spending coincided with the normally heavy July peak in withdrawals and produced a sharp increase in the demand for funds at that time. Associations were able to meet withdrawal requests by drawing on the liquidity reserves they had built up and by borrowing from the Federal Home Loan Banks.

In spite of the extraordinary withdrawal demand which followed the outbreak of hostilities in Korea and which continued for several months, recovery in net savings was rapid and lending volume was maintained at peak levels during 1950. Associations were able to meet the exceptional demands for cash which developed after midyear by using their borrowing power to a greater extent than at any time since the depression of the 1930's. Advances outstanding from the Federal Home Loan Banks and from other banks at the close of 1950 amounted to $891 million as compared with $491 million in 1949. A similar pattern would be expected in any future crisis.

The Federal Home Loan Banks serve as a liquidity backstop for the savings and loan business and for the savers whom the associations serve. The objectives of the Federal Home Loan Bank may be described as follows:

   1) The first duty of the Banks is to provide additional liquidity to the home financing institutions by making advances available to them when an unusual demand for savers' funds occurs. . . .
   2) The second duty . . . is to meet the recurring needs of the members for more loanable funds than the immediate inflow of savings can supply. . . .[1]

Members' demands on the Federal Home Loan Banks for funds are determined by two broad sets of forces. The first set of forces is the balance between mortgage loans made and the sum of mortgage repayments (including prepayments), net savings inflow, and changes in the over-all liquidity of associations. The second set of forces reflects the judgment of savings and loan management as to the degree of liquidity which shall be maintained in an institution. The Federal Home Loan Banks meet these demands for funds by decreasing cash, by decreasing investments, and by increasing flotations of consolidated obligations in the capital markets. Changes in investment holdings of the Banks and changes in the amount of consolidated obligations floated by the Banks have been the major methods through which net demands for funds have been met.

A Management View of Liquidity

The rigid definition of liquidity noted above is not the only basis on which adequacy of cash flows can be measured. Many savings and loan managers find it logical to include receipt of cash from repayments of

---

[1] Twentieth Anniversary Booklet, Federal Home Loan Bank System, 1952.

TABLE 5-3
Sources of Mortgage Lending Funds of Savings and Loan Associations

Source of Funds	Percent of Total Funds		
	June 1960	Oct. 1960	June 1961
Regular monthly payments	43%	39%	38%
New savings	36	44	37
Complete loan payoffs	13	8	14
Prepayments	4	4	5
Borrowings	3	3	4
Other sources	1	2	2
Total	100%	100%	100%

Source: Reports to United States League Committee on Trends and Economic Policies, approximately 120 associations reporting.

loans as an important factor in determining the liquidity of their institutions. To them, liquidity is a flow concept. Table 5-3 lists various sources of cash flows into associations. Mortgage loans turn over, on an average, in six to eight years at savings associations. Taking seven years as the life of the average loan, an association can expect monthly inflow equal to slightly more than 1 percent of the total mortgage loan portfolio. Thus, in a four-month period, cash equal to an additional 5 percent in liquidity will flow into an institution. To the degree that an association has its funds in property improvement loans or shorter-term construction loans, the return flow will be correspondingly swifter. Table 5-4 shows in detail a cash flow worksheet for a typical association.

It is true that the savings and loan business can be defined as a banking operation. Associations do accept money from individuals with the understanding that they will give it back when requested, and they do operate under the banking premise that on any given day, or in any short period of time, only a few people will ask for their money. To that end they must at all times be able to pay those who request their money. But this is not to say that, by the same token, liquidity for savings and loans must be judged by commercial banking tenets. To maintain that loan repayments may not properly be included in the funds needed to meet withdrawal demands is to go back to a banking theory developed prior to the advent of the amortized home mortgage loan made to an individual, and to a theory that flies in the face of the differences in turnover rates between demand deposits and time accounts. If we are to err in liquidity considerations, it is conceded that the error should be on the side of conservatism. But the standard of conservatism should not be that of a demand deposit institution operating in a vastly different market for funds.

Finally, let us consider the concepts of gross and net liquidity from the viewpoint of the total economy. Shifts from one type of asset holding

TABLE 5-4
Illustrative First Half-Year Cash Flow Work Sheet
Typical $15 Million Association

	January	February	March	April	May	June
Total Cash—Beginning of Month	$ 775,000	$912,500	$1,100,500	$1,084,500	$ 980,500	$1,059,000
Add: Cash receipts						
Gross savings receipts	800,000	400,000	400,000	400,000	450,000	400,000
Mortgage loan payments:						
Repayments of principal	115,000	115,000	120,000	120,000	115,000	115,000
Interest collections	45,000	46,000	48,000	50,000	53,000	58,000
Home improvement loan repayments	15,000	16,000	17,000	17,000	17,000	18,000
Proceeds of loans sold	---	---	---	---	---	---
Borrowers' escrows for taxes and insurance	26,000	27,000	28,000	29,000	32,000	33,000
Interest on other investments	1,000	2,000	2,000	1,500	1,750	1,750
Securities maturing	---	---	---	---	---	---
Sale or redemption of securities	---	---	---	---	---	---
Advances from FHLB or bank loans	---	---	---	---	---	---
Miscellaneous	1,000	2,000	2,000	1,500	1,750	1,750
Total cash receipts	$1,003,000	$ 608,000	$ 617,000	$ 619,000	$ 670,500	$ 627,500
Subtract: Cash disbursements						
Savings withdrawals	$ 700,000	$ 250,000	$ 250,000	$ 250,000	$ 200,000	$ 200,000
Cash dividends	---	---	---	---	---	45,000
Christmas club payout	---	---	---	---	---	---
Mortgage loan disbursements	150,000	150,000	160,000	180,000	180,000	180,000
Home improvement loan disbursements	3,500	8,000	10,000	10,000	8,000	8,000
Borrowers' tax and insurance payments	---	---	---	170,000	90,000	30,000
Purchase of securities	---	---	---	---	---	---
Purchase of loans	---	---	---	---	---	---
Repayment of FHLB advances or bank loans	---	---	200,000	100,000	100,000	100,000
Cash operating expenses	12,000	12,000	13,000	13,000	14,000	14,000
Miscellaneous	---	---	---	---	---	---
Total cash disbursements	$ 865,500	$ 420,000	$ 633,000	$ 723,000	$ 592,000	$ 577,000
Total Cash—End of Month	$ 912,500	$1,100,500	$1,084,500	$ 980,500	$1,059,000	$1,109,500

66

to another will not affect the net liquidity of the economy. This can be done only if the Federal Reserve System makes available an increase in the means of payment by increasing the money supply to equal the increase in the demand for money. If the Federal Reserve System were to permit the commercial banks to rediscount mortgages pledged as collateral by savings and loan associations against loans by those banks, then the fullest degree of liquidity would be available to savers at savings and loan associations. Thus, ultimately, the ability of savings associations to have their paper discounted by the Federal Reserve, and the ability of individual savers to become liquid, are contingent upon the ability of the Federal Reserve System to provide the mechanism for discounting various debt instruments through the commercial banking system.

Secular, Cyclical, and Seasonal Influences

One of the most striking characteristics of the American economic system is the steady growth that occurs over several decades. Economists and statisticians use the term "secular trend" to measure this long-term growth. Beneath the trend we find some businesses running well ahead of average and others falling by the wayside. Increase in the demand for a particular good or service is one of the factors which can cause a business to expand faster than does the economy as a whole. Savings and loan associations have more than kept pace with the secular trend. They have grown and prospered in an atmosphere of favorable demand for their product. Two eras of rapid growth have been experienced by savings and loan associations—the 1920's and the period since 1948—both periods of housing shortage and booming residential construction.

There is a definite pattern in the growth of assets, savings, and mortgage loans outstanding since 1900. Two broad thirty-year cycles appear in the average rate of growth and the average dollar growth of assets (Chart 5-1). The first decade of the thirty-year cycle was marked by slow growth or loss, speed picked up in the middle period, and the final ten years were characterized by rapid growth. There were losses (negative growth) in all categories in the decade of the 1930's.

Savings and loan associations are recognized as institutions which promote thrift in order that home financing funds can be accumulated. As the demand for such services rises, the intensity with which savings are solicited increases and the volume of savings rises. The shape of the curve in Chart 5-2 indicates that savings at savings associations are now in a period of very active growth. The straight-line trend line indicates no tendency for growth of savings to level off. A theory advanced by R. B. Prescott some years ago may be of interest here. According to Prescott, there are four stages of growth: (1) a period of experimentation during which there is only a small amount of growth, (2) a period of

CHART 5-1

POPULATION, SAVINGS, AND INCOME IN THE UNITED STATES, 1900 - 1960
PER CAPITA INCOME, 1929 - 1960

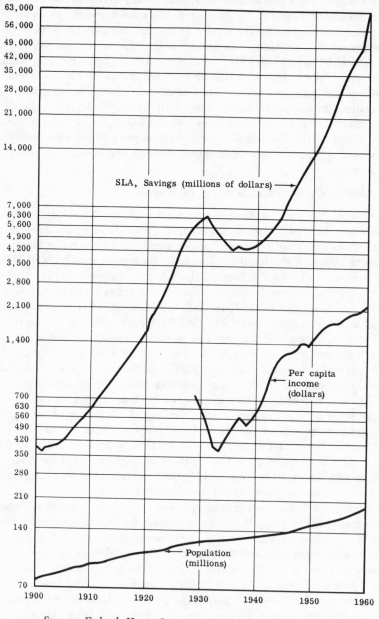

Source: Federal Home Loan Bank Board, U.S. Department of Commerce.

growth, (3) a period during which growth occurs at a slower pace as the saturation point is approached, and (4) a period of stability.[2] In such a context, associations probably are not yet through phase two, but signs of phase three appear in a number of sub-regions across the nation.

CHART 5-2

SAVINGS AT SAVINGS AND LOAN ASSOCIATIONS 1900 - 1958

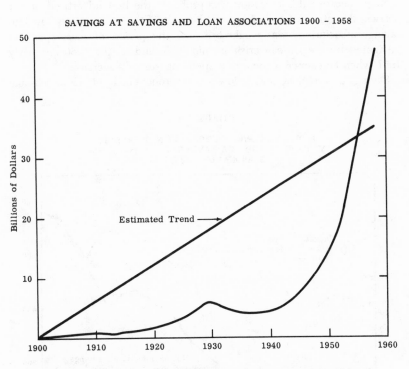

Source: Partly estimated from data contained in H. Morton Bodfish, ed., *History of Building and Loan in the United States* (Chicago, 1931); Federal Home Loan Bank Board, 1930-60.

Savings and loan savings are affected by fluctuations in the business cycle, although variations in this area do not follow the business cycle as closely as do other elements in the economy. In fact, the relationship appears to be an inverse one (Chart 5-3). The periods of expansion and contraction in the general business cycle, as determined by the National Bureau of Economic Research, are also indicated on this chart. Peaks and troughs in industrial production conform much more closely to the NBER indicators than do variations in savings and loan savings. Savings

_____

[2] Raymond B. Prescott, "Law of Growth in Forecasting Demand," *Journal of the American Statistical Association,* XVIII (December 1922), 471-479.

tend to exhibit a countercyclical pattern, particularly during periods of contraction in general business. They rise most strongly, it appears, when the economic outlook darkens and consumers become more cautious and turn their sights from spending toward saving. During postwar years, gains in savings were greatest when recessionary forces held sway—1949, 1953-54, and early 1958. The 1958 reaction was especially noticeable, perhaps because this recession was probably the best advertised of our postwar downturns. Looking at the other side of the coin, savings flow into savings associations was weakest during the period of mass spending instigated by the Korean crisis in mid-1950, and during 1956 and early 1957 when consumer income and spending steadily increased.

Savings and loan savings follow a very pronounced pattern of seasonal

CHART 5-3

INDUSTRIAL PRODUCTION AND NET SAVINGS
AT SAVINGS AND LOAN ASSOCIATIONS 1947 - 1959
SEASONALLY ADJUSTED

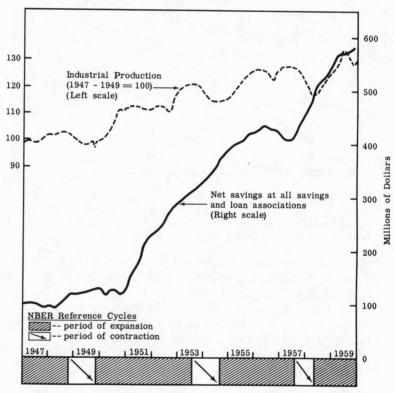

Source: Federal Home Loan Bank Board, Federal Reserve Board, National Bureau of Economic Research.

variation (Chart 5-4). Peaks in gross savings occur in January and July, the reinvestment periods following payment of dividends. The top months for net savings are June and December, when withdrawals are lowest in anticipation of dividend payments and when dividends are

CHART 5-4

INDEXES OF SEASONAL VARIATION, GROSS AND NET SAVINGS
AT SAVINGS AND LOAN ASSOCIATIONS

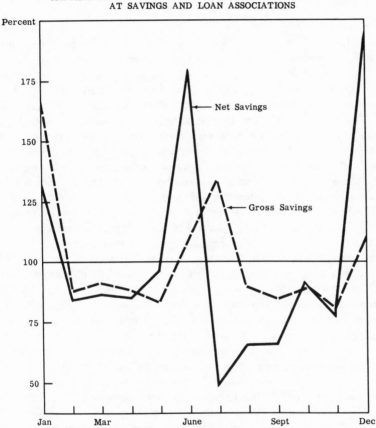

Source: Based on data of the Federal Home Loan Bank Board for 1946 to 1958.

credited to accounts.[3] Appendix B explains the method of adjusting data for such seasonal variations.

---

[3] The increasing number of associations paying dividends quarterly is causing a shift in the relative importance of April and October in the seasonal pattern.

Safety

Savers' funds at savings and loan associations are protected by several means:

1) Pursuance of prescribed and standardized mortgage lending policies and other investment procedures,
2) Holding of liquid assets,
3) Reserves for losses, and
4) Federal insurance of accounts.

Through the years, various laws have been placed on both state and federal statute books to protect the public interest in matters of savings and loan association operations. Government agencies have been created to administer these laws and to see that their provisions are carried out. They ascertain through various examination procedures that the individual associations are functioning according to the law and that the records of the individual associations present fairly the facts on operations. They have the further responsibility of advising the respective legislative bodies of needs if and when new laws or modifications of existing laws are deemed advisable. Through this combination of statutory and administered law the public interest is safeguarded.

The basic protection for savers' funds at savings associations rests in the quality of the mortgage loan assets and other investments acquired by the individual institution and management's care in the selection of borrowers, performance of credit checks on such borrowers, and appraisal of property acquired. The safeguards here are much like those exercised in lending operations by other financial institutions. Certain rules of thumb have been developed in the business and generally are applied.

Some critics maintain that the safety in a savings and loan account, resting as it does on a portfolio of mortgage loans, can be sustained only in strong real estate markets such as those of the 1950's, and that these markets have served to create an illusion regarding safety that could very well disappear in a "more normal" economic climate. Such critics fail to give sufficient credit to the features that have been built into the mortgage lending business and the American economy since the 1930's.

Virtually all mortgage loans today are amortized on a monthly basis. For the mortgage borrower, this makes the mortgage payment similar to a monthly rent payment, and equates the payment terms of the contract with the time period in which the typical borrower receives his salary. In addition, the rising levels of personal income in this country have made possible a growth in accumulated savings among average families, so that many home buyers now have a greater reserve fund to fall back on should their regular income cease. Broad built-in stabilizers such as unemployment insurance also work to make a monthly mortgage payment a surer claim than it used to be. Such structural developments enhance basic safety of the savings and loan association as a savings medium.

These and other features serve to provide a far greater degree of safety in the investment portfolio of savings and loan associations, and consequently in the liabilities of such institutions, than was true at any time in the past. Looking to the future, the trend seems to indicate a further enhancement of the safety features of associations during the years to come.

Holdings of Liquid Assets

Savings and loan associations are legally required to maintain strict liquidity holdings of cash and United States government securities equal to 7 percent of total savings and investment accounts. (Effective January 1, 1961, the Federal Home Loan Bank Board raised this requirement from 6 percent to 7 percent.) Actually, savings associations hold, on the average, a considerably greater percentage of liquid assets than the required minimum. Assuming the strictest legal definition of liquidity, at the end of 1960 their liquid assets equaled 12 percent of their total savings capital. Adding "secondary" liquidity holdings such as Federal Home Loan Bank debentures, FNMA obligations, and similar investments, total liquidity amounted to 13 percent of capital accounts.

It is true that the liquid asset holdings of savings and loan associations have decreased since the end of World War II. The decrease, however, was less pronounced in the case of associations than it was in the case of mutual savings banks or insurance companies. Associations now have considerably more of their funds in liquid form than was true prior to the depression of the 1930's. Savings and loan management has very definite feelings regarding liquidity. As a matter of course, managers operate on the premise that there must always be sufficient funds in highly liquid form to pay savers' withdrawal requests. In addition, they are quite concerned about the need for having sufficient funds on hand to meet responsible requests for home financing. The motivation here is partly psychological. Association managers seem convinced that word must not get around that their association is "short of cash" or does not have the money to make a quality home loan. Partly for this reason, liquidity holdings of associations are, on the average, double the legal requirement now in force. The psychological aspect of the holdings of liquid assets is especially important in smaller communities where word of mouth is the customary method of spreading news.

Reserves

Through the years, savings and loan associations have built up a reserve fund to protect their savers against possible losses. These reserves are a capital cushion to absorb unusual losses that cannot be absorbed by current earnings. They differ from the reserves placed by member commercial banks at their regional Federal Reserve Banks. At the end of 1960, total reserves of savings and loan associations averaged 8 percent of savings capital. As Table 5-5 shows, the reserve ratios declined between 1950 and 1955; this decline was due to extremely rapid growth of savings capital. Since 1955 they have changed little, for even though growth has continued strong, additions to reserves have kept pace.

TABLE 5-5
Reserves[1] as a Percentage of Savings Capital
All Savings and Loan Associations
1940–1960

Year	Reserve Ratio	Year	Reserve Ratio
1940	10.9%	1950	9.4%
1941	10.4	1951	9.4
1942	10.4	1952	8.9
1943	10.2	1953	8.6
1944	9.5	1954	8.3
1945	9.1	1955	8.1
1946	9.2	1956	8.1
1947	9.1	1957	7.9
1948	9.2	1958	8.0
1949	9.2	1959	8.0
		1960	8.0

[1]The term "reserves" refers to various capital funds set aside to absorb unusual losses and includes surplus and undivided profits.

Source: United States Savings and Loan League, based on data of the Federal Home Loan Bank Board.

Under a formula adopted by Congress in 1951, savings and loan associations are permitted to deduct a "reasonable addition to a reserve for bad debts." The formula for determining a "reasonable addition" is as follows: An amount determined as reasonable by the taxpayer, but not to exceed the lesser of (1) the amount of taxable income, or (2) the amount by which 12 percent of withdrawable accounts at the end of the year exceeds the sum of surplus, undivided profits, and reserves at the beginning of the year. The present formula for determining reserves for losses, applicable to both savings associations and mutual savings banks, was adopted by Congress in the light of testimony by impartial supervisory authorities, and reflects the. distinguishing features of these institutions as compared with commercial banks.

The commercial banks determine their "reasonable addition" to reserves for losses on a formula developed by the United States Treasury Department. That formula permits additions to reserves of an amount determined as reasonable by the taxpayer; no addition, however, is to result in total reserves exceeding three times an amount determined by multiplying outstanding loans at the end of year by the average ratio of bad debt losses to outstanding loans during any twenty-year period after 1927.

Another point worthy of note is that mutual institutions, unlike commercial banks, may accumulate reserves only through retained earnings. If savings associations are to weather periods of economic stress, such reserves must be built up gradually from earnings during prosperous periods, in advance of possible and inevitable losses.

Savings and loan law requires associations to build up reserves on a progressive basis over a prescribed period of time. The Federal Savings and Loan Insurance law states that after twenty years of operation, an association must have accumulated a reserve equal to 5 percent of savings capital. The Insurance Corporation has also developed a series of bench marks which must be met by individual institutions in building toward this requirement; associations must reach this 5 percent figure according to a specified schedule by the twentieth anniversary of their founding. If an association falls behind this build-up schedule, it must place 25 percent of net income into reserves each year. After its twentieth anniversary, it must place 10 percent of net income into reserves each year, and if its reserve position falls below 5 percent after the twentieth year, 25 percent of net each year must go into reserves.

Insurance of Accounts

Title IV, added to the National Housing Act in 1934, provided for the establishment of the Federal Savings and Loan Insurance Corporation to insure the safety of savings accounts in savings and loan associations. The Corporation, which is self-supporting, provides a maximum insurance of $10,000 per account. At the end of 1960, more than twenty-seven million persons in 4,098 associations (with 93 percent of the assets of the business) held insured savings accounts. All savings and loan associations operating under federal charters are required to be members of the Federal Savings and Loan Insurance Corporation, and membership is also available to state-chartered institutions which apply and qualify for membership.

The Federal Savings and Loan Insurance Corporation has as its sole function the protection of the safety of savings accounts in savings and loan associations. When the proper public supervisory authority or a court of competent jurisdiction (depending on the association's charter) declares an insured institution to be in default, the insurance becomes operative. The Corporation also has broad preventive powers to aid an association in the first stages of difficulty. For example, when an association is faced with a critical financial situation, the Insurance Corporation may come to its rescue by purchasing its assets or by making a cash contribution or loan.

The law specifies the procedure to be followed when the Insurance Corporation pays out on insured accounts in the event of default and liquidation. When the proper state or federal supervisory authority assumes charge of an insured savings association declared in default, the Insurance Corporation makes an immediate determination of the holders of the accounts, notifies them and returns their savings funds up to the maximum insurance of $10,000. The provisions for settlement, as amended by Congress in 1950, parallel closely the provisions of the Federal Deposit Insurance Corporation.

The State of Massachusetts enacted legislation for the establishment of its own insurance fund in March 1934, four months before Congress authorized the establishment of the Federal Savings and Loan Insurance Corporation. The Massachusetts program is compulsory for all cooperative banks and the state-chartered mutual thrift and home financing institutions in the state.

The Rotation Principle

The savings contract of the majority of savings and loan associations permits these institutions to repay funds to savers under a rotation plan if serious economic stress should prevent payment on other bases. The law specifies that when an association is unable to pay all withdrawal requests within a period of thirty days from the receipt of written request for such withdrawals, the institution shall number and file such requests in the order received and shall proceed in the following manner: Withdrawal requests shall be paid in order received. If any holder of a savings account has requested the withdrawal of more than $1,000, he shall be paid $1,000, and his withdrawal request shall be charged with such amount as paid. His request shall then be renumbered and placed at the end of the list of withdrawal requests. Thereafter, when his request is reached, he shall be paid a like amount and shall continue to be so paid until his request is paid in full. Although the specifics of the rotation scheme may vary from state to state, the basic principles are quite similar.

Savings associations have the right to pay the withdrawal value of savings accounts at any time upon application, and since the 1930's have been doing so as a matter of course. If the amount is not paid within thirty days, however, the rotation plan shall take effect.

The rotation principle is of long standing in the savings and loan business, and was designed to equate the terms of the savings liability contract with the nature of the assets in which these savings are invested. The purpose was to avoid auction-block liquidation of savings and loan assets at a time when the market for such assets was demoralized, by making possible the more orderly liquidation of assets at terms more acceptable to the institution and its members. In many respects, in our modern financial world, the rotation plan is of only historical interest. The safety features built into the economy and into the savings and loan business during the last generation have tended to reinforce the premise that the rotation plan could be eliminated without harm, a conviction held by a good many savings and loan executives and Federal Home Loan Bank System officials. In fact, there is sentiment at the federal level as well as in a number of states for removing rotation from the settlement provisions in savings and loan account contracts. Practitioners in the business maintain that little or no change need be made in portfolio composition or investment powers and privileges if the legal possibility of rotation is eliminated from savings contracts. The State of New York made such a change for its state-chartered associations in 1958.

Tax Differences and Savings Flows

The tax laws of the United States recognize that fundamental differences exist between taxpayers. Individuals and corporations are taxed differently. Among corporations themselves essential differences exist as far as the application of income tax law is concerned. Extractive industries, such as oil companies and mining firms, receive an allowance based on the depletion of resources of that particular company. This allowance can be related to the length of time the specific resource may be expected to remain in existence.

A broader type of time allowance exists in the case of depreciation. Although the general rules for depreciation of assets are similar across industry lines, exceptions are not uncommon. The most notable of these exist in national defense type industries where accelerated write-offs are permitted because of the specialized character of assets which become obsolete in a very short time.

One pervasive element in all these illustrations is that, in the interest of equity, the exceptions are based on the differences between the actual time it takes to use up specific assets and the ordinary taxable year. To put it another way, the tax accounting period, ordinarily taken as twelve calendar months, does not coincide with the "natural" acounting period or asset life. Reserve allowances are based on estimates and expectations of the normal life of the assets in question and the time interval which must pass before the assets are to be replaced or completely used up. Broad assumptions based on past knowledge and expectations regarding the estimated life of the specific assets are basic to equity.

These principles aid our understanding of the differences which exist between the taxation techniques used for commercial banks and those used for savings associations. Savings associations making home mortgage loans for periods of fifteen, twenty, and twenty-five years must be considered quite differently from commercial banks making short-term business loans for one, three, and six months. At commercial banks, the lending process, including complete repayment, is completed within a twelve-month period and profit or loss can then be determined. For savings associations the period involved before similar determinations can be made is substantially longer. The tax law affecting savings and loan associations takes these differences into consideration. It does this under the principle of equity, interpreted to mean that taxpayers in equal circumstances should be taxed equally.

Equity also demands that measures should be taken to equate differences in the essential character of various enterprises through reserves for depreciation or losses so that equal taxation is possible. To tax all financial institutions on the same basis in the interests of "equal taxation" would be grossly inequitable and would fail to give proper credit to the distinguishing features of the various institutions. It would be similar to permitting depreciation allowances on precisely the same basis for all manufacturers of transportation equipment. This would mean that automobile manufacturers, railroad equipment manufacturers, aircraft manufacturers, and missile makers would have equal depreciation allowances. In the field of finance this principle was recognized in the tax law for life insurance companies. Any such scheme developed in the interest of tax equality would create and foster gross inequities in itself.

Present Taxing Formula

Savings associations are subject to the same corporate income tax rates and the same general regulations applying to all major financial institutions including commercial banks. The one significant difference is in the way savings associations are permitted to determine deductions for additions to bad debt reserves in computing taxable income. From an equity standpoint, the primary point of contention is the bad debt reserve allowance permitted savings associations, and which banks are not permitted.

Under a formula adopted by Congress in 1951, savings associations are permitted to deduct for additions to bad debt reserves an amount determined as reasonable by the taxpayer, but not to exceed the lesser of (1) the amount of taxable income, or (2) the amount by which 12 percent of withdrawable accounts at the end of the year exceeds the sum of surplus, undivided profits, and reserves at the beginning of the year. Commercial banks are permitted to compute deductions for additions to bad debt reserves based on a multiple of the average loss experience of individual institutions during any twenty-year period since 1927 on commercial bank holdings of eligible loans. The Treasury Department determines the commercial bank reserve formula.

Since such associations cannot sell stock, the accumulation of adequate reserves at mutual thrift institutions can be accomplished only through retained earnings. Reserves are built up gradually from earnings during prosperous periods in advance of expected losses. Such reserves should permit savings associations to withstand periods of serious economic stress. Since 1951, associations have built their reserve for losses from $1.5 billion to $5.0 billion, holding their reserve ratios to savings capital fairly steady. This has been done despite the tremendous growth in new savings at their institutions and pressures for home financing funds.

The Need for Reserves

The record of the past thirty years indicates how difficult it is to build up protective reserves from earnings. During the 1930's and during World War II, the lengthy process of writing off and absorbing large depression losses on mortgage loans hampered the build-up of reserves at savings associations. This was true despite the drastic cuts in the dividends paid to savers and in correspondingly sharp increases in the proportion of earnings retained. Following the war, the build-up of adequate reserves was also difficult because of rising dividend rates and large gains in savings capital. Competition for savings was intensified and rates of return on all thrift and investment accounts rose considerably. Savings associations paid these higher rates of return to all savers so that a continued inflow of funds needed to support home building might be maintained. Rates of earnings of savings associations increased more slowly than the return paid to savers because a considerable proportion of their assets were locked into low-yield, long-term mortgages and government securities acquired at lower interest rates during earlier years.

The establishment of the 12 percent of savings capital in the bad debt reserve formula adopted by Congress in 1951 was based in part on the recommendations of state banking supervisory authorities. The banking supervisors in many states advised Congress that mutual thrift institutions needed reserves of 13 percent to 15 percent of savings capital for the protection of savers in periods of economic stress. The depression experience of savings associations recounted in Chapter 9 of this monograph supports such a contention.

Advocates of reductions in bad debt reserve allowances of savings associations point to the increased role of the federal government in economic stabilization, and to other built-in structural changes in our economy, as factors working to lessen the extent of future business recessions and the need for reserves for losses on the part of financial institutions. In part, such contentions have merit. It is unlikely that future business recessions will be as severe or as prolonged as the Great Depression of the 1930's. Certainly the mortgage contract has been improved by such features as regular amortization, FHA insurance, VA guarantees, and other devices. At the same time, loan-to-value ratios have been increased quite liberally and maturities have been lengthened. Furthermore, mortgage lending volume reached a peak at a time when real estate prices hit all-time highs. A full and complete assessment of these factors and their impact on the risk of loss at financial institutions holding such debt instruments is difficult, to say the least. The weights an individual gives to these various factors may well be the prime determinant of the reasonableness of a 12 percent bad debt reserve figure.

A critical question, then, is: How is one to determine the weights for these factors in a tax formula, and what assumptions are to be the basis of these weights? At this writing it appears that the most appropriate guide is the historical record of the 1930's. Reserve building at associations is designed to protect savers against the possibility that future events may bring to this economy a catastrophe of similar proportions. Reserves of 12 percent would have permitted financial institutions in the home financing field to pass through the 1930's reasonably well. As evidence, we offer the relatively more favorable depression experience of mutual savings banks, whose reserves totaled 11 percent of savings deposits, as compared with savings and loan associations, whose reserves in 1930 totaled 4 percent of savings capital.

Conclusion

Consideration of the questions of tax reform regarding savings and loan associations should recognize these facts: Savings associations are subject to regular corporate income tax rates and the same general income tax regulations as all other financial institutions, including commercial banks. The one exception is in the treatment of the bad debt reserve. Here, consideration of the length of the time cycle involved in savings and loan lending operations as contrasted to commercial bank lending operations must be given extremely close scrutiny. The tax laws should not be used as a device whereby commercial banks may compete more effectively for savings under a kind of price control arrangement. Finally, one of the vital needs of the American economy is the stimulation of savings for the financing of capital formation. Thus, there is reason to encourage, rather than impose a penalty upon, institutions designed specifically to stimulate thrift in the interest of sustainable economic growth without inflation. The home financing needs of the American public seem to have a high priority in our society. The present methods of meeting those needs could not be made more efficient if present tax proposals are adopted.

Chapter 6

ROLE IN THE
INVESTMENT PROCESS

Investment Trends

The primary investment objective of savings and loan associations is to broaden home ownership. Legally, associations may invest in relatively few assets: one- to four-family home mortgages, United States government securities, Federal Home Loan Bank debentures, municipal bonds in certain states, and, to a limited extent, property improvement loans, first mortgage loans on commercial properties, churches, land development, etc. An examination of the trend in savings and loan assets by type of investment reveals that the investment mix at associations has changed little since 1950. Association managers apparently have achieved a balance in their operations which they feel is quite suitable, given today's housing and capital markets and existing lending powers. Since 1950, approximately 78 percent of savings and loan assets have been invested in one- to four-family mortgages. Variations in this percentage have been slight; a high of 79.9 percent was reached in the peak housing year of 1955 and a low of 77.8 percent in the recession year 1958. Cash and Governments make up the second largest holding.

The trend in savings and loan investments by general type for the prewar and postwar periods may be seen in Table 6-1. Total assets of associations rose from $8.7 billion in 1945 to over $70 billion at year-end 1960. Practically all the increase went to support home ownership. In percentage terms, total mortgage holdings, including holdings other than on one- to four-family homes, increased from 61 percent of total assets in 1945 to 84 percent of total assets in 1960. Government bond holdings, although rising in total dollars, declined in percentage terms from 28 percent of total assets in 1945 to 6 percent in 1960.

In part, the concentration of assets in mortgages yielding somewhat higher rates than corporate or government securities permitted savings associations to pay the rate of return required to attract larger amounts

81

TABLE 6-1
Trends in Investments of Savings and Loan Associations
1939-1960

(Millions of Dollars)

Type of Investment

Year	Mortgages 1- to 4-Family Homes	Estate Owned[1]	U.S. Government Bonds	Cash	Other Mortgages	Property Improvement Loans	Other Assets[2]	Total Assets
1939	$ 3,616	$689	$ 73	$ 274	$ 190	$ 59	$ 696	$ 5,597
1940	3,919	499	71	307	206	64	667	5,733
1941	4,349	332	107	344	229	61	627	6,049
1942	4,349	206	318	410	234	42	591	6,150
1943	4,355	117	853	465	229	30	555	6,604
1944	4,617	60	1,671	413	183	31	483	7,458
1945	5,156	33	2,420	450	220	41	427	8,747
1946	6,840	26	2,009	536	301	81	409	10,202
1947	8,475	13	1,740	560	381	130	388	11,687
1948	9,841	12	1,455	663	464	171	422	13,028
1949	11,117	15	1,462	880	499	206	443	14,622
1950	13,116	21	1,489	951	598	217	454	16,846
1951	14,844	13	1,606	1,082	766	247	606	19,164
1952	17,645	21	1,791	1,306	771	326	725	22,585
1953	20,999	20	1,923	1,500	958	391	847	26,638
1954	25,004	24	2,005	1,962	1,084	448	981	31,508
1955	30,001	33	2,319	2,085	1,353	538	1,204	37,533
1956	34,004	42	2,743	2,116	1,715	625	1,536	42,781
1957	37,996	51	3,154	2,163	1,973	720	1,996	48,053
1958	42,890	74	3,785	2,571	2,588	839	2,231	54,978
1959	49,587	104	4,477	2,183	3,607	960	2,612	63,530
1960	55,883	120	4,586	2,715	4,201	1,100	2,884	71,489
		As Percent of Total Assets						
1939	64.6%	12.3%	1.3%	4.9%	3.4%	1.1%	12.4%	100.0%
1940	68.4	8.7	1.2	5.4	3.6	1.1	11.6	100.0
1941	71.9	5.5	1.8	5.7	3.8	0.9	10.4	100.0
1942	70.7	3.3	5.2	6.7	3.8	0.7	9.6	100.0
1943	65.9	1.8	12.9	7.0	3.5	0.5	8.4	100.0
1944	61.9	0.8	22.4	5.5	2.5	0.4	6.5	100.0
1945	58.9	0.4	27.7	5.1	2.5	0.5	4.9	100.0
1946	67.0	0.3	19.7	5.3	3.0	0.7	4.0	100.0
1947	72.5	0.1	14.9	4.8	3.3	1.1	3.3	100.0
1948	75.5	0.1	11.2	5.1	3.6	1.3	3.2	100.0
1949	76.0	0.1	10.0	6.0	3.4	1.5	3.0	100.0
1950	77.9	0.1	8.8	5.6	3.4	1.3	2.9	100.0
1951	77.5	0.1	8.4	5.6	4.0	1.1	3.3	100.0
1952	78.1	0.1	7.9	5.8	3.4	1.4	3.3	100.0
1953	78.8	0.1	7.2	5.6	3.6	1.5	3.2	100.0
1954	79.4	0.1	6.4	6.2	3.4	1.4	3.1	100.0
1955	79.9	0.1	6.2	5.6	3.6	1.4	3.2	100.0
1956	79.5	0.1	6.4	4.9	4.0	1.5	3.6	100.0
1957	79.1	0.1	6.6	4.5	4.1	1.5	4.1	100.0
1958	77.8	0.1	6.9	4.7	4.7	1.5	4.3	100.0
1959	78.1	0.2	7.0	3.4	5.7	1.5	4.1	100.0
1960	78.2	0.2	6.4	3.8	5.9	1.5	4.0	100.0

[1]Excludes office buildings

[2]FHLB stock, buildings, equipment, etc.

Source: Federal Home Loan Bank Board; United States Savings and Loan League.

of money into their offices. Associations today, as in 1939, follow an investment philosophy of placing every dollar possible in the home mortgage market. What some observers regard as the limited investment powers of associations has not disturbed most association executives. In fact, the power to invest only in mortgages seems to have worked in their favor during the housing boom of the postwar years. During the years ahead, savings associations will no doubt continue to place the bulk of their funds into home mortgages. This is the investment medium managers know best and, as long as opportunities to lend exist there, they will continue to concentrate in home loans. Expansion of investments into areas outside the general field of shelter are not now being advocated broadly among savings association executives. Increased penetration of shelter markets other than single-family homes, however, may come.

Virtually all financial institutions came out of the war with one common investment characteristic: All were heavily loaded with federal government securities. They began to shift away from such obligations into higher-yielding investments during the latter 1940's. Mortgages, particularly the government-backed variety, were regarded with steadily increasing favor by almost all lending institutions. Not only did new funds flow into mortgages from savings associations, but also from insurance companies, mutual savings banks, and to some degree, commercial banks as well. Despite a general shift of funds into the mortgage field, savings associations have dominated the home mortgage lending market during the postwar period as few institutions have dominated any other sector of the capital market.

Based on what we know today, the mortgage market should continue to retain and perhaps even further enhance its position relative to other sectors of the capital markets during the next decade. In all probability, the housing field will remain constantly before the eyes of Congress, and Congress will probably see to it that a continuing large flow of funds finds its way into housing.

Investment Portfolios and Cycles

Little evidence of a secular shift in the trend of investment portfolio composition can be seen at savings associations. Mortgages continue to be preferred almost exclusively. On a cyclical basis, associations do tend to increase the share of their cash flows placed in mortgages during peak building years such as 1950, 1955, and 1959. The optimal balance which association executives seek between savings inflows and loan demand outflows on a current basis is rarely achieved. Holdings of liquid assets are the adjustment mechanism used to correct the imbalances which appear. Analysis of the year-end data on savings, lending, and liquidity demonstrates this fact (Table 6-2). Since 1948, the peak years in mortgage loan demand were years in which net inflows from savings declined.

TABLE 6-2
Major Sources and Uses of Funds
All Insured Savings and Loan Associations
1950-1959
(Millions of Dollars)

	Major Uses of Funds				Major Sources of Funds				
Year and Quarter	Mortgage Loans Closed	Liquidity Increase	Other Uses	Total Uses	Net Savings Receipts	Loan Repayment and Prepayments	Liquidity Decrease	Other Sources Including FHLB Advances	Total Sources
1950 - 1st	$ 869	$ 40		$ 909	$ 396	$ 441		$ 72	$ 909
2nd	1,198	37		1,235	437	567		231	1,235
3rd	1,273			1,273		699	$ 203	371	1,273
4th	1,012	195		1,207	499	488		220	1,207
	$ 4,352	$ 272		$ 4,624	$1,332	$2,195	$ 203	$ 894	$ 4,624
1951 - 1st	$ 1,004			1,004	280	634	20	70	1,004
2nd	1,189	107		1,296	568	597		131	1,296
3rd	1,164			1,164	385	592	69	118	1,164
4th	1,144	240		1,384	664	630		90	1,384
	$ 4,501	$ 347		$ 4,848	$1,897	$2,453	$ 89	$ 409	$ 4,848
1952 - 1st	1,178	101	$ 33	1,312	656	656			1,312
2nd	1,520	99		1,619	776	707		136	1,619
3rd	1,617			1,617	496	780	60	281	1,617
4th	1,533	267		1,800	908	849		43	1,800
	$ 5,848	$ 467	$ 33	$ 6,348	$2,245	$2,992	$ 60	$ 460	$ 6,348
1953 - 1st	1,486	109	95	1,690	830	860		196	1,690
2nd	1,888	145		2,033	966	871		264	2,033
3rd	1,934	221		1,934	561	957	152	6	1,934
4th	1,676			1,897	1,027	864			1,897
	$ 6,884	$ 475	$ 95	$ 7,554	$3,384	$3,552	$152	$ 466	$ 7,554

84

Table (rotated on page; columns are unlabelled on this page). Values by year and quarter:

1954	1st	1,588	146	113	1,847	978	869		131	1,847
	2nd	2,065	208		2,273	1,171	971		373	2,273
	3rd	2,254			2,254	677	1,101	103	99	2,254
	4th	2,269	351		2,620	1,326	1,195			2,620
		$ 8,176	$ 705	$113	$ 8,994	$4,152	$4,136	$103	$ 603	$ 8,994
1955	1st	2,317	130		2,447	1,053	1,150		244	2,447
	2nd	2,949	129		3,078	1,365	1,332	◆308	381	3,078
	3rd	2,953			2,953	612	1,400		633	2,953
	4th	2,200	516	232	2,948	1,538	1,410			2,948
		$10,419	$ 775	$232	$11,426	$4,568	$5,292	$308	$1,258	$11,426
1956	1st	2,205	146	117	2,351	1,054	1,269		28	2,351
	2nd	2,651	131		2,899	1,476	1,423			2,899
	3rd	2,606		252	2,606	651	1,382	203	370	2,606
	4th	2,233	432		2,917	1,527	1,390			2,917
		$ 9,695	$ 709	$369	$10,773	$4,708	$5,464	$203	$ 398	$10,773
1957	1st	2,084	122	21	2,227	980	1,247		397	2,227
	2nd	2,569	169	73	2,811	1,507	1,304			2,811
	3rd	2,632		195	2,632	465	1,460	310		2,632
	4th	2,283	419		2,897	1,590	1,307			2,897
		$ 9,568	$ 710	$289	$10,567	$4,542	$5,318	$310	$ 397	$10,567
1958	1st	2,106	280	158	2,544	1,258	1,286		200	2,544
	2nd	2,849	447		$ 3,296	1,719	1,377	135	696	$ 3,296
	3rd	3,344	439		3,344	826	1,687		26	3,344
	4th	3,262			3,701	1,964	1,711			3,701
		$11,561	$1,166	$158	$12,885	$5,767	$6,061	$135	$ 922	$12,885
1959	1st	3,099	141		3,240	1,337	1,696		207	3,240
	2nd	4,096	210		4,306	2,022	1,806		478	4,306
	3rd	4,073	313	160	4,073	998	1,921	394	760	4,073
	4th	3,310			3,783	2,004	1,779			3,783
		$14,578	$ 664	$160	$15,402	$6,361	$7,202	$394	$1,445	$15,402

Source: Based on data of the Federal Home Loan Bank Board.

As a result, associations fell back on liquidity and on their ability to secure advances from the Federal Home Loan Bank System to honor commitments.

Chart 6-1 shows the relationship between annual changes in net savings capital and new mortgage loans made year by year along with the corresponding adjustments in liquid assets. In years when lending activity rose during the 1950's, savings flow slowed and association managers compensated for this by adding less to government security holdings. In

CHART 6-1

YEAR TO YEAR VARIATIONS IN SELECTED MEASURES
AT SAVINGS AND LOAN ASSOCIATIONS, 1948 - 1959

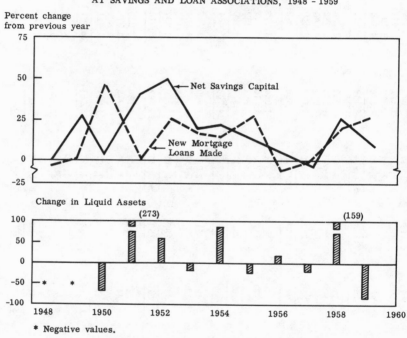

Source: United States Savings and Loan League.

other years, when loan demand slowed, savings gains tended to pick up, permitting a rapid build-up in liquid asset holdings at associations. The years 1951, 1954, and 1958 are outstanding cases in point. Since this chart was based on year-end data, it may well hide the true turning points in investment decisions over the cycles. Nevertheless, a consistent pattern does emerge.

Data on sources and uses of funds by quarters (Table 6-2) may point up more accurately the manner in which the savings and loan business tends to equate the demand for loans with available sources of funds. Peak home building years 1950, 1955, and 1959 were also years when liquidity gains slowed and other sources of funds, principally FHLB advances, were drawn upon heavily. In 1959, for example, "other sources" of funds accounted for 9.4 percent of total funds used, as against 3.7 percent of total funds used in 1956 and 1957. Net savings gains accounted for approximately 40 percent to 45 percent of total sources of funds during the 1950's. In 1950, however, when associations were faced with the heavy withdrawals accompanying the Korean War buying spree, only 29 percent of total funds came from net savings. Liquid assets, FHLB advances, and other sources made up the balance.

Unlike commercial banks, which to a very large extent create deposits out of lending operations, savings associations must have a dollar of cash on hand to make a dollar of loans. When the supply of funds flowing in from savings receipts, mortgage loan repayments, and net income earned by the association, or generated through the conversion of liquid assets, falls short of the demand for funds from mortgagees, associations can turn to their regional Federal Home Loan Banks for advances and to other sources of borrowable money. Such borrowings are employed by associations to equate demand and supply imbalances on a cyclical as well as a seasonal basis.

Seasonal Aspects

As mentioned earlier, the flow of funds at savings and loan associations has a rather pronounced seasonal character. Loan repayments are received in a relatively steady flow throughout the year, but net savings inflow tends to concentrate most heavily in two months—June and December. Lending volume is heaviest during the peak building season from May through August. The normal seasonal pattern is shown in Chart 6-2. In this chart we see the excess or deficiency of savings and loan flows month by month compared with a hypothetical normal month. Typically, the deficiency of funds is heaviest in the third quarter when savings inflow is lowest and loan demand is high. The largest excess occurs in the winter months when savings receipts are high but loan closings tend to level off. Association managers attempt to estimate as accurately as possible the seasonal cash flows as a guide to establishing a balance between savings flow and lending flow, and to making adjustments in liquidity to compensate for the variations between savings inflow and mortgage loan demand. Given this seasonal flow, recourse is made to Federal Home Loan Bank credit in order to maximize investment opportunities.

Analysis of the sources and uses of savings and loan funds on a quarterly basis points up the manner in which adjustments are made in liquid

CHART 6-2

INDEXES OF SEASONAL VARIATION

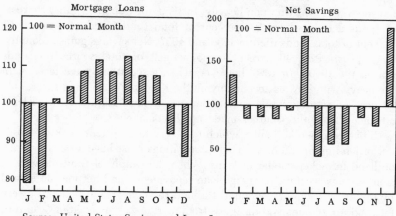

Source: United States Savings and Loan League.

asset holdings and other sources of funds, primarily Federal Home Loan Bank advances, to compensate for imbalances in money flows into and out of savings associations (Table 6-2). In all ten of the third quarters between 1950 and 1959, outflow exceeded inflow and liquid assets were sold to support loan operations. In the other three quarters of each year an opposite pattern was in evidence, with a liquidity build-up taking place.

Summary

Savings and loan associations concentrate their investments almost exclusively in the one- to four-family residential property mortgage loan. In placing their funds into such long-term investments, they find that years of peak building and real estate activity tend to be years in which the dollar inflows from mortgage repayments and net gains in savings do not quite equal the total demand for funds. Under such circumstances, savings associations look first to their liquid asset holdings of cash and government securities and attempt to make appropriate adjustments. If these do not cover their requirements, Federal Home Loan Bank System members may turn to their regional Banks for advances to smooth out the imbalances. When demand pressures rise, associations take action in the loan market as well, seeking to ration credit by tightening loan terms and raising interest rates and by becoming more selective in their commitments to builders. If the imbalance of funds becomes extreme, the individual associations may be forced to withdraw from the lending market temporarily.

Home Mortgage Lending

Mortgages on one- to four-family residential properties comprise the bulk of savings and loan assets (Table 6-1)—78 percent of total assets of associations are in this type of investment at the present time. Mortgage debt outstanding at savings associations has increased approximately twelvefold since the end of World War II. In the nation as a whole, mortgage debt on one- to four-family non-farm houses during the same period grew from $18.6 billion to $141.7 billion, or 762 percent. Of this $141.7 billion of mortgage debt at the end of 1960, over $118 billion was held by financial institutions. Savings associations held 47 percent of it, compared with 42 percent in 1945.

Savings associations specialize in the conventional type of mortgage loan as distinguished from government backed loans, namely FHA and VA mortgages. Of the $60.1 billion of savings and loan assets in mortgages at the end of 1960, only $7.2 billion represented VA loans and $3.5 billion FHA loans. On a percentage basis, approximately 81 percent of the mortgage loans held were of the conventional type, 13 percent were VA's and 6 percent were FHA's.

FHA Loans

Savings and loan associations have never been heavy users of the Federal Housing Administration home mortgage lending program. Table 6-3 shows the proportion of FHA insured mortgages in total mortgage holdings for each major mortgage lending institution for the years 1946-60. Savings and loan associations have never held more than 6.2 percent of their mortgage funds in FHA contracts. Furthermore, since 1950, associations have been reducing the proportion of FHA loans in their portfolios. Since 1958, however, when the yields on FHA loans became more attractive, holdings of such contracts by associations have risen slightly.

Although some individual associations in a few cities do make considerable use of the FHA program, the number is small, and such institutions usually have special reasons for the type of operation they conduct. Major builders working in low priced home markets, for example, may have traditionally offered low down payment properties to the community and be reluctant to operate in any other way. In general, the smaller the association, the less use it makes of FHA.

Part of the explanation as to why savings associations have been reluctant to use FHA lies in the nature of savings associations and their historical development. Associations are almost exclusively local home mortgage lending institutions, gearing their operations to the local community and typically holding to maturity any mortgages they originate.

TABLE 6-3
FHA Mortgage Holdings of Major Lenders
As Percentage of Their Total Home Mortgage Holdings
1946–1960

Year-End	Savings Associations	Life Insurance Companies	Mutual Savings Banks	Commercial Banks
1946	6.1%	43.5%	14.2%	29.7%
1947	4.8	36.6	12.0	22.1
1948	5.5	41.3	16.5	23.1
1949	6.2	45.7	18.0	25.2
1950	6.2	43.4	23.4	26.5
1951	5.7	38.8	28.9	27.4
1952	5.0	37.1	28.9	28.4
1953	4.9	35.4	27.4	29.3
1954	4.6	31.7	24.8	28.5
1955	4.6	28.9	23.2	28.4
1956	4.3	26.7	22.3	27.8
1957	4.2	25.7	22.2	26.7
1958	4.8	20.1	23.6	21.5
1959	5.6	21.1	25.1	21.8
1960	5.9	23.3	29.1	28.7

Sources: 1946-56: "The Volume of Mortgage Debt in Postwar Decade," Saul B. Klaman, National Bureau of Economic Research. 1957-60: Federal Reserve Board.

(Until very recently the sale of mortgages by savings associations was virtually unknown.) Savings associations aim to provide fast and efficient mortgage lending service. Because they are restricted to the one- to four-family first mortgage loans and to a fifty-mile primary lending radius, they have usually tailored their operations to meet the specific requirements of their local market. Since the end of World War II, most institutions have found the demand for mortgage funds running ahead of the supply of savings, and the typical institution had not fully cultivated its own fifty-mile lending market.

The purpose of the FHA program was primarily to promote employment in the construction industry during the 1930's by encouraging financial institutions to put up the money to support home lending. The goal was to be accomplished by encouraging the making of higher loan-to-value advances and longer-term mortgages, standardizing the mortgage contract, improving its marketability, and moving toward a national market for mortgage paper. Such provisions were not needed by savings associations in order to make loans in the 1930's, and they are not necessary or particularly attractive today in developing a large volume of home loans. Federal savings and loan associations, for example have had the right to make conventional loans up to 80 percent of appraised value since 1935 and up to 90 percent since 1958. The FHA loan, with its standardized nature and government guarantee, is of greatest value to the lender who invests in mortgages over a wide area or who buys loans from others. Since associations are not typically buyers and sellers of mortgages, and exist primarily to serve the needs of local markets, the aspects of the FHA loan giving it marketability and removing the necessity of lender inspection of the details of each loan have been of little use or interest to savings associations.

The FHA lending-rate ceiling was thought by many to be the principal reason for opposition to FHA lending on the part of savings and loans during the 1930's. In 1934, for example, associations were paying a dividend of 4.5 percent to 5 percent, and the FHA lending rate ceiling was set at 5 percent. Later, when events brought the cost of money down as low as 2 percent and 2.5 percent, associations still did not move into the FHA program. This may indicate that the fixed rate was not the only reason the savings and loan business never embraced the government insurance plan.

Administrative requirements under FHA, so-called "red tape," are another factor working against participation in FHA by savings associations. FHA lending requires familiarity with a substantial number of regulations and administrative procedures. There may also be time delays under FHA in the handling of contracts. Such hurdles can be overcome most effectively by an institution having in its employ a highly organized clerical staff that can process a considerable number of contracts with similar characteristics. The size of the typical savings association and the relatively limited number of employees on its staff generally make impractical the establishment of a separate FHA department. A typical association with $10 million in assets handles 100 mortgage loans per year. If 25 percent of these were FHA contracts, this would mean 25 FHA loans per year, or about 2 per month, probably well below the number required to warrant participation in the program.

There are also some very real ideological reasons for the reluctance of the savings and loan business to embrace the FHA program. A great many savings and loan managers simply do not believe that government should in any way be involved in the risks of home mortgage lending. They feel that federal insurance or guarantee ordinarily has no place in their business, and consequently choose to avoid the use of such programs. Only time will tell whether such a philosophy will be maintained at a time when the supply of available loanable funds exceeds by a substantial margin the demand for conventional loans. Changing market conditions have been known to alter managerial judgments quickly.

The VA Program

The attitude of savings and loan managers toward the VA program, however, has been quite different. Associations were glad to have the opportunity to participate in this move by the federal government to make it easier for veterans to obtain housing, and were probably the first institutions to embrace the VA program on a large scale. Savings which had been invested in government bonds by associations during the war because of low demand for mortgage loans, were available to move in volume into VA guaranteed loans. From the beginning of the VA program in 1944 until the end of 1959, savings associations made $12.1 billion in VA mortgage loans—almost 25 percent of all such loans. In 1960 they did 21 percent of the total VA volume, second only to mortgage companies.

The simplicity of the VA program compared with the FHA program appealed to association managers. In addition to decentralized control, the program's automatic guarantee feature provided for prompt cash settlement of claims filed after default. The record for defaults in the case of VA guaranteed home loans has generally been favorable.

The greatest activity on the part of associations in VA loans occurred during the 1950's. After building up to a peak of approximately $1.6 billion in VA loans during 1955, the volume slowed. Savings and loans added only $422 million in VA loans to their books in 1960. The decline was due to the high level of interest rates in the mortgage market, which discouraged lenders from extending VA guaranteed credit at sub-market rates, and to the decline in the number of eligible ex-servicemen.

Investments Other Than Home Loans

Government Securities

United States government securities are the second most important investment of savings associations. These securities may readily be converted into cash and are considered part of the basic liquidity of the institution. As mentioned earlier, because mortgage lending opportunities were severely curtailed along with home building during World War II, associations built up substantial holdings of government securities (Table 6-1).

Savings and loan associations, unlike other financial institutions, did not hesitate in their movement out of government bond investments into mortgages following World War II. Within six years, from 1945 to 1950, they had cut their government holdings to 8.8 percent of total assets, one-third their wartime size. In dollars, holdings declined from $2.4 billion to $1.5 billion despite the sizable growth of associations. It is a safe assumption that virtually all these assets were converted into one- to four-family mortgage loans. At mutual savings banks, insurance companies, and commercial banks, the liquidation was similar but took a little longer to accomplish.

Investment in government securities and other legal instruments is relatively simple for savings and loan associations because of their re-stricted powers. In the case of federal associations, the only alternative to direct federal government issues is investment in FNMA debentures and notes or Federal Home Loan Bank consolidated notes. In the typical association, the bond account is not large enough to warrant the em-ployment of a full-time executive to handle it. The task usually becomes the responsibility of the managing officer, although he sometimes finds it very difficult to keep abreast of the ever-shifting money markets and the resulting changes in yields and prices.

Certain state-chartered savings associations have the right to purchase municipal bonds (federally chartered institutions do not have this power), but have done so in relatively limited volume. In any period characterized by a strong demand for mortgage loans and a lesser volume of savings, associations will exhibit relatively little interest in municipal bonds. In addition, under existing tax provisions, they would be paying for a tax exemption having little meaning for them. Despite present limited interest in municipals, broadening the powers of savings asso-ciations to include such investment floated to improve community facili-ties and for other purposes related specifically to housing would be in keeping with the basic objectives of the savings and loan business.

Savings associations generally adhere to a policy of investing for income rather than for price appreciation. They consider their bond in-vestments as liquidity, and speculation in the government bond market as not advisable. This does not necessarily mean, however, that the in-stitution may not take advantage of price and yield differentials or the buying of new issues which may be priced better than current yields. One procedure strongly recommended for associations is to establish a ladder of maturities in their government bond holdings. Such a spaced-maturity program provides the association with an average return on its bond investments over a complete business cycle. The sophistication of association executives in the management of liquid assets is growing.

In recent years there has been an adequate supply of high-grade mortgages available to savings associations. Thus, the primary function of investments in Governments has not been as an alternate investment opportunity, but rather have they been made for liquidity purposes. As mortgage maturities have lengthened, government security investments have become shorter and shorter. Because the average association's in-vestment in government securities is relatively small, the difference in over-all return between long-term and short-term holdings is not great. Of greater importance is the fact that with shorter-term maturities in a portfolio, associations can assure themselves of stable income over the years, plus real liquidity. In making such investments, they leave specu-lation to the bond dealers.

Table 6-4 shows the changes in the composition of government securities held by savings associations between 1955 and 1960. The pattern in the holdings of government securities by savings associations has shifted from longer maturities to shorter-term bills, certificates, and notes. Although this trend was tempered somewhat in 1959 under the attraction of relatively higher yields in the five-year range of the market, the direction is clear.

Commercial Mortgages and Other Investments

Other investments, individually and as a group, are of minor significance at savings and loan associations. They include loans on residential structures of more than four families; churches; commercial properties

TABLE 6-4

Types of U.S. Government Securities Owned by Savings and Loan Associations
as of December 31, Selected Years
(Percentage Distribution)

Type of Security	1955	1957	1958	1959	1960
Treasury bills	4.4%	8.0%	5.7%	7.8%	6.4%
Certificates	1.0	5.6	2.3	2.0	2.2
Notes	4.1	10.1	10.6	16.7	19.8
Bonds to maturity:					
1 year and under 5 years	4.3	23.7	19.2	28.3	21.0
5 years and under 10 years	21.3	6.0	16.3	17.2	17.3
10 years and under 20 years	33.1	28.9	24.2	13.1	13.0
20 years and over	3.8	3.7	10.6	8.2	15.8
Convertible bonds	5.4	3.9	2.8	2.3	2.4
Savings bonds	22.6	10.1	8.3	4.4	2.1
Total	100.0%	100.0%	100.0%	100.0%	100.0%

Source: Based on reports to the United States Savings and Loan League from institutions representing approximately 40 percent of total savings and loan assets.

such as bowling alleys, motels, and commercial store properties; property improvement loans; and land development loans. The interest in and amount of such lending varies widely at individual institutions. Mortgages on properties other than one- to four-family homes comprise the largest "other investment" holding, accounting for approximately 5 percent of savings and loan assets. Unsecured property improvement loans (including FHA Title 1 loans) made up approximately 1 percent of savings and loan assets during the 1950's. Funds may be advanced for such purposes through other techniques as well, such as the reopening of an existing mortgage loan and the use of the open-end mortgage. The category "other assets" also includes investment in Federal Home Loan Bank stock, office building, equipment, and the like.

Participation Loans

A technique authorized in 1957, whereby one savings and loan association may participate in loans made by another association is growing in importance. Under this plan an association may purchase up to 75 percent of an individual residential mortgage loan made and serviced by another institution whose accounts are insured by the FSLIC, regardless of the location of the property securing the loan. The program started slowly but is now picking up considerable momentum (Table 6-5). The

TABLE 6-5
Participation Loans Bought and Sold by Insured Savings and Loan Associations
From Beginning of Program through December 31, 1960
(Thousands of Dollars)

Sales

	First Quarter	Second Quarter	Third Quarter	Fourth Quarter	Total[1]
1957[2]					$ 36,306
1958	$28,732	$30,604	$ 29,136	$55,754	144,226
1959	46,642	59,691	61,350	37,278	204,961
1960	41,525	79,849	111,036	86,470	318,880

Purchases

	First Quarter	Second Quarter	Third Quarter	Fourth Quarter	Total[1]
1957[2]					34,919
1958	31,406	28,470	29,198	53,263	142,337
1959	49,276	54,269	54,412	36,198	194,155
1960	38,950	75,054	104,741	89,005	307,750

[1]The total amount of sales does not exactly equal the total amount of purchases in any one period because of differences in time in the reporting of participation activity.
[2]Last nine months of 1957; regulations authorizing program were issued on March 29, 1957.

Source: Federal Home Loan Bank Board.

bulk of the sales of participations is being made by institutions in the Southeast and on the West Coast and the heavy buying is being done by associations in the East and Northeast. The purpose of this program is to help equalize the supply of and demand for money in different communities and regions by facilitating the transfer of funds from areas where savings are accumulating faster than loan demand to areas where loan demand exceeds available funds.

One type of participation transaction deserves special mention. Suppose a new industry moves into a small community and creates a new and sizable demand for home financing which the local associations cannot handle. Through the use of participations, this small town association may be able to meet local loan demand, hold and supervise these loans locally, and keep increased traffic coming through its doors. Without the participation program, this could not be accomplished by a small, local institution. It probably would have to stand aside and watch a distant mortgage banker or insurance company move in and do the financing job. Competition in the local mortgage market is thus increased to the benefit of the ultimate home purchaser. This arrangement is analogous to what the big city commercial banks have been doing for many years for their small-town correspondent banks on all types of loans.

Federal associations have clear-cut authority to buy and sell participations. This authority, however, has not been granted by all of the states to state institutions. State-chartered associations in some states can neither buy nor sell participations, while others can sell but not buy. In some states where participations can be sold, such sales are surrounded by restrictions more limiting than the federal regulations. A recent change in regulations allows federal associations to invest a full 20 percent of assets in participations alone, provided the amount of participations and other loans that normally come under the 20-percent-of-assets limitation do not exceed 30 percent of assets.

Basic Factors Governing Investment Policies of Savings Associations

As basically mutual thrift and home financing institutions, savings and loan associations have developed a strong public service *raison d'être*. They hold that their basic purpose is to serve the shelter needs of the American people. Theoretically, they operate under the premise that they pay too much for money and have excessive operating expenses. Such feeling serves to focus management attention on ways of obtaining ample funds at a lower cost. Associations strive constantly to improve the competitive position of the conventional loan and to broaden home ownership among American families. Yet, as far as the general public is concerned, associations are identified primarily as thrift institutions rather than as home lenders. In addition, much, if not most, of the promotional effort of associations is on the side of savings solicitation. How can we explain this apparent inconsistency?

Thoughtful savings and loan executives state that aggressive thrift solicitation happens to be the most economical method by which large pools of funds can be assembled and made available to mortgage borrowers. They defend the relatively higher rates offered to savers on the premise that such rates are necessary to encourage sufficient savings at their institutions so that the existing home loan demand may be served. They believe that it is preferable to expand home ownership by having an ample supply of mortgage funds available at what may appear to be relatively high rates than to have insufficient dollars available at lower rates.

Tradition in the Savings and Loan Business

Tradition plays an important part in the investment activities of any financial institution. Despite the fact that the savings and loan business has fewer traditions than banks or insurance companies, executives in the business do hold definite attitudes which affect their operations and which may be classed as traditions.

The Concept of Growth. The concept of growth has come to be a tradition in the savings and loan business. Savings and loan executives believe that the growth of their institutions is necessary to serve the public interest. An increasingly mobile and growing population needs continuous access to home mortgage funds for both new and existing homes. When individual communities have their own pools of savings available for home mortgage loans, they are not entirely dependent on far-away lenders and the local market is usually better served. The need for homes on the part of American families, the congressional attitude toward supplying funds for home purchases, and the dangers inherent in giant-sized federal direct-lending programs and public housing developments have tended to spur associations to grow large enough to meet the demand for home financing funds from private savings.

Growth has been widespread among savings associations and has not been concentrated in a few institutions. At times, savings and loan executives tend to rate each other on the basis of the asset size or the relative growth of their respective institutions. Managers whose institutions have grown rapidly and who have mastered the art of digesting growth on the run, so to speak, seem to command the respect of fellow managers. The growth of physical facilities, savings sources, lending opportunities, employee staffs, and so on, are manifestations of the superior ability of the specific institution to serve the people in its community and to meet the public welfare objectives of the institution.

One of the adjustments ahead for savings and loan management must be the realization that growth comparable to that which has taken place over the past ten years will be more difficult to achieve. For one thing, the very size of savings associations will tend to limit opportunity for appreciable percentage gains in the future since the base from which managers must work will be larger. In addition, associations in the past have grown not only with the demand for their services but also by taking business away from competitors, on both the savings side and the lending side of the business. Many institutions now find their major competition coming, not from other financial institutions in savings and mortgage markets, but rather from other savings associations competing on much the same terms as they do. They are finding that individual associations paying comparable rates on savings and offering comparable mortgage contracts at competitive rates make considerably tougher competitors than do other types of financial institutions.

Future growth may be tied more closely to community growth and external forces than it has been since World War II. As marginal lenders leave the area, the ability of associations to capture business from other financial institutions will be reduced. As this is realized, management may well intensify efforts to further industrial and commercial growth in the community so as to increase income, savings, and potential mortgage borrowers. Savings and loan managers also recognize that the larger their institution becomes, the greater is its ability to compensate those on the executive staff responsible for the services rendered by that institution. Since most institutions are mutual in character, these factors—the growth in responsibility and earning assets—become highly important motivations to management.

Permanent Home Loans. A very real tradition among savings and loan associations is the preference for keeping rather than selling home mortgage loans originated by the institution. Association managers prefer to stay "at home" in their lending operations. In many instances they do not fully cultivate even the fifty-mile radius permitted under FSLIC regulations. In addition, association executives generally feel that home loans, once made, ought to be retained by the individual association until repayment, that the relationship between the borrower and the financial institution ought to be continuous, and that the buying and selling of loans should be a relatively minor part of savings and loan operations. Management also tends to look askance at unsecured loans, and this fear may help to explain why property improvement lending has not been undertaken in greater volume by associations.

Basic Investment Objectives

The investment objectives of savings and loan management regarding maturity, liquidity, yield, and safety are interrelated. Because they confine themselves to mortgage investments by law, by choice, and by tradition, association managers do not concern themselves with the relative yields and attractiveness of alternate investment holdings as does a commercial banker, life insurance company officer, or other investor who can exercise considerable discretion in this area. The yield on mortgage loans, typically, is determined by market forces in the money and capital markets of the country, usury laws, and administered rate ceilings, as well as the association management.

The sensitivity of mortgage interest charges to national monetary conditions is most apparent in the larger cities and in the more competitive financial centers. In smaller towns across the country, where mortgage lending opportunities are relatively limited, the interest charges on mortgage loans tend to vary much less from one phase of the business cycle to another. At some associations every loan ever made bears a 6 percent interest rate.

Ideally, association managers seek to secure from their mortgage investments a yield sufficient to cover dividends paid to savers, operating expenses, and the building up of reserves for the protection of savers. A rule of thumb held in the past called for a 2 percent spread between dividend rates and mortgage rates. Loans would be made at 6 percent, for example, and dividends to savers would be paid at a 4 percent rate. Recent years have seen this "ideal" spread narrow to 1.5 percent. In the business, the phrase "squeeze on earnings" is used to describe the pressures narrowing the spread. Automation and various economies are one answer. The use of fees, commissions, and charges has been another.

Mechanics of the Investment Process

The savings and loan business is a relatively simple one as far as investment procedures are concerned. A parallel exists between the department store and specialty shop in retailing and the commercial bank and the savings association in finance. The savings and loan is the specialty shop of home financing.

Investment Activity at Smaller Associations

At small associations, a single individual may function as the managing officer, savings officer, and chief loan officer. Such an association would have only seven to ten employees and its assets would be under $10 million. Of the 6,200 savings associations in the country, 4,465 are under $10 million in asset size. In 1960, these associations held total assets of approximately $14 billion, or 20 percent of total savings and loan assets.

Typically, in the day-to-day operations of the smaller institutions, loan applications are submitted to the managing officer. Often a backlog of loan demands can be found at smaller institutions. Appraisals are made either by members of the board of directors or by independent appraisers on a fee basis. Considerable emphasis is placed on the reputation of the person applying for the mortgage and the builder doing the construction, as well as the knowledge the savings and loan officer may have of the real estate market in his community. A loan approval committee consisting of the managing officer and several directors may take formal action on loan applications. A typical $10 million association processes and makes approximately 100 new loans a year, and services a portfolio of approximately 600 loans. Loans are held to maturity or cancellation, and the buying and selling of loans is undertaken only on rare occasions.

The manager also handles the liquid asset portfolio of the association, and the pattern in this account will depend on the investment abilities and preferences of that manager. Some small institutions may keep all of their liquid funds on deposit with their Federal Home Loan Bank; others may hold only Treasury bills; still others may have a quite carefully selected and individually supervised portfolio of liquid assets.

Unsecured home improvement loans may be made on an individual

CHART 6-3
AN ORGANIZATIONAL HISTORY, SAGINAW SAVINGS

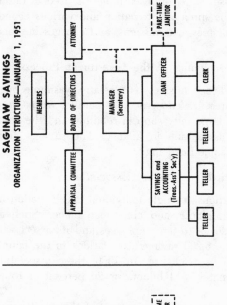

SAGINAW SAVINGS
ORGANIZATION STRUCTURE—JANUARY 1, 1951

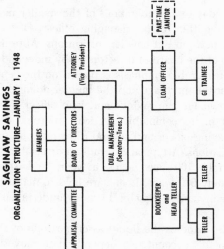

SAGINAW SAVINGS
ORGANIZATION STRUCTURE—JANUARY 1, 1948

Organization, mission, structure, functions, and personnel changed little in the three-year period from January 1, 1948, to January 1, 1951. One teller was added as association grew less than $1 million in these years, had not hit $5-million asset mark when new manager took helm on January 1, 1951. Attorney continued dual manager role in advisory capacity until June 30, 1951, and, interestingly, employee shown as GI trainee and clerk today is Saginaw Savings' second man

—vice president in charge of the loan department. Most obvious drawback to association's service to the community and growth was dismal storefront-type office. While location was reasonably good, there was absolutely no customer appeal to cramped, poorly lighted quarters. Says oldest employee in point of service: "It was like spending twenty-three years in a dungeon."

(*Continued*)

100

CHART 6-3 (Continued)

In these two organizational charts we see the impact of the progressive policies and objectives set by the board of directors and new management. Between January 1, 1951, and January 1, 1956, Saginaw Savings grew more than threefold, from assets of $4,481,600 to $14,639,300. Biggest factor was a new location and building, completed in August 1952. Note some degree of departmentalization and specialization as of January 1, 1953, when assets had attained $7,612,600. By January 1, 1956, three major operating areas—savings, lending, and accounting—had been departmentalized and most employees were performing specialized duties.

(*Continued*)

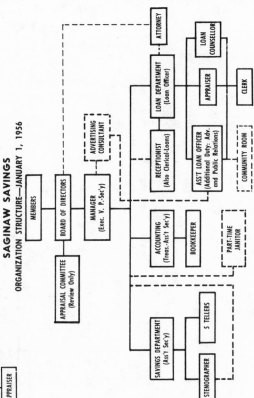

SAGINAW SAVINGS
ORGANIZATION STRUCTURE—JANUARY 1, 1956

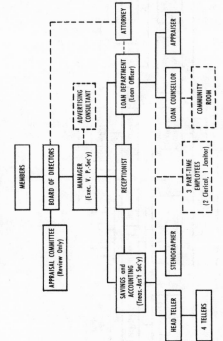

SAGINAW SAVINGS
ORGANIZATION STRUCTURE—JANUARY 1, 1953

CHART 6-3 (Continued)

By year-end 1958 (assets $21,049,300) the association had been organized into four departments, and management had delegated to department heads all operating responsibility except liquidity, Government securities portfolio, Saginaw Savings' subdivision development activity, and key personnel matters.

(Continued)

SAGINAW SAVINGS
ORGANIZATION STRUCTURE—JANUARY 1, 1959

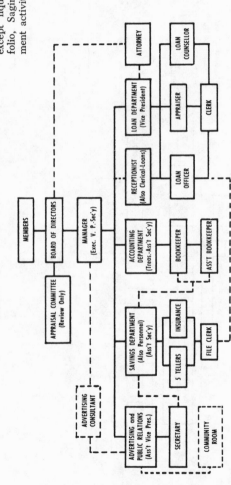

102

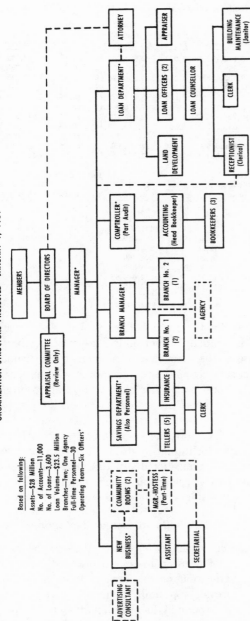

SAGINAW SAVINGS

ORGANIZATION STRUCTURE PROJECTED—JANUARY 1, 1961

Based on following:

Assets—$28 Million
No. of Accounts—11,000
No. of Loans—3,600
Loan Volume—$23.5 Million
Branches—Two; One Agency
Full-time Personnel—30
Operating Team—Six Officers*

MEMBERS

BOARD OF DIRECTORS

APPRAISAL COMMITTEE
(Review Only)

MANAGER*

ATTORNEY

LOAN DEPARTMENT*

APPRAISER

LOAN OFFICERS (2)

LAND DEVELOPMENT

LOAN COUNSELLOR

CLERK

RECEPTIONIST (Clerical)

BUILDING MAINTENANCE (Janitor)

COMPTROLLER* (Part Audit)

ACCOUNTING (Head Bookkeeper)

BOOKKEEPERS (3)

BRANCH MANAGER*

BRANCH No. 1 (2)

BRANCH No. 2 (1)

AGENCY

SAVINGS DEPARTMENT* (Also Personnel)

TELLERS (5)

INSURANCE

CLERK

NEW BUSINESS*

COMMUNITY ROOMS (2)

MGR.-HOSTESS (Part-Time)

ASSISTANT

SECRETARIAL

ADVERTISING CONSULTANT

CHART 6-3 (Continued)

With its first branch now under construction and scheduled for opening on or about October 1 of this year, a second branch and an agency (loans only) in the planning stage for 1960, Saginaw Savings' organization structure should look something like this on January 1, 1961. Association will be completely functional and specialized. Note, particularly, land development specialist, leaving manager even more free to plan, supervise, direct, make major decisions, work with management team and on policy matters with members of the board of directors.

(*Continued*)

CHART 6-3 (Continued)

SAGINAW SAVINGS' TEN-YEAR OPERATING RECORD

Year-End	Assets	No. of Savings Accounts	Savings	No. of Loans	Loan Amount Outstanding	Liquidity (% of Savings)	Gross Income
1948	$3,609,994.46	2,175	$ 3,112,172.68	1,057	$ 2,581,752.33	26.3%	$ 127,772.50
1949	3,905,568.85	2,129	3,353,802.17	1,147	2,868,291.29	25.4%	149,752.63
1950	4,481,619.88	2,258	3,600,435.47	1,274	3,590,273.58	19.5%	173,217.46
1951	5,775,982.96	2,608	4,652,863.71	1,363	4,457,150.62	20.2%	221,339.60
1952	7,612,658.76	3,684	6,835,396.48	1,551	5,811,923.73	14.8%	287,656.14
1953	10,090,160.97	4,640	8,998,732.02	1,826	7,670,904.44	16.1%	386,346.22
1954	12,012,688.22	5,403	10,728,509.41	2,107	9,684,201.84	11.4%	514,251.15
1955	14,639,289.49	6,550	13,030,222.98	2,393	11,979,973.34	10.4%	632,752.53
1956	16,840,413.07	7,346	14,945,016.83	2,576	13,204,305.63	13.3%	753,982.97
1957	19,078,745.48	8,138	16,806,889.45	2,726	14,412,602.51	15.8%	900,967.59
1958	21,049,291.33	8,448	18,463,861.21	2,879	16,226,557.58	14.5%	1,142,779.50

Year-End	Operating Expense	Operating Ratio (Expense to Gross Income)	Addition to Reserves	Total Reserves	Percent of Reserves to Assets	No. of Persons Per Million $
1948	$ 36,410.98	28.4%	$ 28,919.90	$ 361,020.77	10.0%	1.9
1949	37,952.19	25.3%	30,649.48	391,670.25	10.0%	1.8
1950	46,384.04	26.7%	39,962.09	431,632.34	9.6%	1.8
1951	67,411.66	30.4%	55,387.63	487,019.97	8.4%	1.3
1952	87,925.70	30.5%	79,962.72	566,982.69	7.4%	1.4
1953	95,722.45	24.7%	107,277.72	674,260.41	6.6%	1.3
1954	118,913.88	23.1%	160,637.87	834,898.28	7.0%	1.2
1955	130,828.11	20.6%	219,788.57	1,054,686.85	7.2%	1.1
1956	149,383.95	19.8%	248,246.74	1,302,933.59	7.7%	.95
1957	170,008.98	18.8%	250,436.02	1,553,369.61	8.0%	.94
1958	175,150.34	15.3%	380,886.11	1,934,255.72	9.1%	.90

basis to existing customers, but these transactions probably will not be large in volume. Smaller institutions do not undertake great numbers of construction loans because of the specialized character of such lending. They are more likely to concentrate on the financing of existing properties or of new homes after the construction has been completed. Mortgage warehousing, participations in loans originated by others, buying and selling of loans, and FHA lending activity are rarely, if ever, undertaken at the smaller associations. The mortgage commitment process is relatively less important at smaller institutions that do not deal directly with builders. Chart 6-3 shows the organizational structure of a typical small association and the evolutionary development which comes with growth. The key point during the early stages is the simplicity of the structure.

Investment Organization and Activity at Larger Institutions

As a savings and loan association increases in size, the complexity and departmentalization of its operations increase. Generally, the first departmentalization is the segregation of the savings function and the lending function. Loan approval, appraisal, servicing, processing, and collection work is usually incorporated in one department. Electronic data-processing equipment may be employed to handle both mortgage and savings accounts. Such equipment is considered suitable when an association has reached an asset size of $50 million to $75 million. The

CHART 6-4

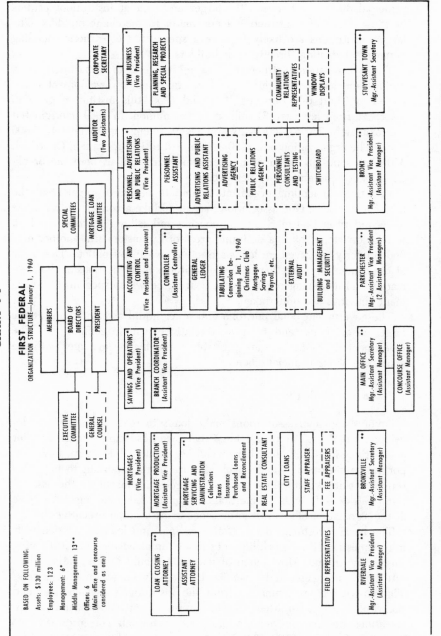

FIRST FEDERAL
ORGANIZATION STRUCTURE—January 1, 1960

BASED ON FOLLOWING:
Assets: $130 million
Employees: 123
Management: 6*
Middle Management: 13**
Offices: 6
(Main office and concourse considered as one)

ORGANIZATIONAL STRUCTURE, ASSOCIATION OVER $100 MILLION IN ASSET SIZE principal difference between the larger and smaller institutions centers in the volume of construction loans made to merchant builders. The larger institutions are likely to have a specialized construction lending department dealing directly with builders.

The organizational structure of a mortgage loan department at a savings and loan association at various stages in its development is depicted in Chart 6-3. Between 1948 and 1959, this institution grew in asset size from less than $1 million to $21 million. In 1959 it originated approximately 250 to 300 loans and was servicing approximately 2,800 loans. The organization of a $130 million institution appears in Chart 6-4. Although some of the functions performed are similar, here the breakdown is considerably more detailed.

Variations in lending organization tend to be more prevalent at the larger institutions. One association may undertake a considerable volume of secondary market mortgage purchasing and selling; another may look to land development as a desirable area for expansion; still another may find property improvement loans attractive investment outlets. The needs of the community, together with the aptitudes and traditions of the association and its management, have a bearing on which specialized investment activities are undertaken.

The government bond portfolio and other liquid asset holdings at the larger associations tend to have a relatively simple composition. The investment decisions here are probably made by the manager with the assistance of his financial officer.

Managing Cash Flows

Savings and loan associations make loans to real estate brokers, developers, builders, and individual borrowers seeking funds. Smaller associations find individual borrowers, i.e., walk-in borrowers, more important, while builders and developers are more important to big institutions seeking volume loan outlets. In almost all instances, the association deals directly with the mortgage borrower. Loan closings take place at the association offices in the presence of association executives.

The basic investment decision at a savings and loan association rests in the question: How much liquidity should an association have? Turning this query around: How much of its assets should an association place into home mortgages and other fixed, relatively long-term investments? The answer comes ultimately from the institution's management and board of directors. In attempting to determine portfolio distribution, associations devote considerable time, either formally or informally, to cash flow forecasts. Table 6-6 shows a typical liquidity computation for an association with $10 million of assets and $8.7 million in withdrawable savings capital. By making a series of assumptions, managers come

TABLE 6-6
Illustrative Liquidity Computation

		Amount	% of Savings
Withdrawable savings capital		$8,700,000	
Cash on hand and in banks	$300,000		
U.S. Government obligations—			
less pledged amount	$600,000		
FHLB certificates of deposit	$150,000		
LEGAL LIQUIDITY		$1,050,000	12.0%
FHLB and FNMA notes	$125,000		
TOTAL QUICK ASSETS		$1,175,000	13.5%
Loans in process—set up on books	$100,000		
Borrowers' escrow accounts	$ 50,000		
Short-term savings accounts	$200,000		
Loans—expected to be closed shortly	$150,000		
(Not in loans in process)			
Principal and interest to be paid within			
90 days on advances and borrowed money	$ 50,000		
Other current liabilities including			
accounts payable	$ 10,000		
TOTAL CURRENT LIABILITIES		$ 560,000	6.5%
NET QUICK ASSETS		$ 615,000	7.0%

up with a cash flow worksheet for the first six months of a hypothetical year.[1]

The typical association holds a little more than 3 percent of association assets in cash on hand and in banks. This percentage, being an average, may not hold for individual associations. Each institution's need for cash varies according to the day-to-day business it must handle. Bank balances to cover check payments, and compensatory balances required by commercial banks under reciprocal arrangements to reimburse them for services rendered, may also alter the percentage. In general, however, associations tend to carry somewhat larger balances than are necessary in commercial banks. Such balances could be profitably invested with little or no effect on an association's day-to-day transaction requirements.

Many managers realize that gross liquidity equivalent to 6 percent of withdrawable accounts—the legal requirement in 1960—is insufficient for transactions. The amount of liquidity required at an institution can be determined only from estimates of future needs for funds based on the record of past experience and on the management's assessment of the business climate. The technique most often used here is to develop a projection of future cash needs through a cash flow worksheet such

---

[1] The basic data in this illustration are taken from statistics compiled by the United States Savings and Loan League in the spring of 1960 and are based on reports from over 1,400 association managers in all parts of the country.

as is shown in Table 5-4. The elements enumerated provide an understanding of the factors considered by savings and loan management in determining liquidity needs.

Management feels the safety and availability of funds placed with its institution rests on these elements: (1) a flow of new savings; (2) monthly mortgage repayments; (3) cash and securities; (4) mortgage loans that can in any normal period be sold by one type of institution to another institution of the same type, or by one type of institution to another type of institution, (mortgage loans are not completely illiquid assets, even though associations by choice and for their own purposes hold them until maturity or cancellation); (5) the reserves of the institution; (6) the ability of the association to borrow from the Home Loan Banks to meet any seasonal or unusual cash demands; and (7) a portfolio of good, carefully made home loans in properties in the area.

Chapter 7

INFLUENCE OF GOVERNMENT POLICY
ON SAVINGS FLOW AND
INVESTMENT PROCESS

The Impact of Monetary Policy

The purpose of this chapter is to assess the impact of monetary policy on the operations of savings and loan associations. Such an evaluation, however, is difficult and hazardous, for monetary climate is only one of many factors which affect any single sector of the economy. The conclusions reached are based upon an examination of data for the period 1951-59. That period was chosen because the Federal Reserve System did not operate effectively as an independent agency in the field of monetary control prior to 1951; until the spring of 1951, Federal Reserve policy worked to support and stabilize the market for government securities. While the period covered by the survey is short, it does include two business cycles in which monetary authorities pursued alternating policies designed to confine cyclical variations within reasonable limits.

The method employed was to examine variations in the financial position of savings associations relative to swings in the business cycle and the actions of Federal Reserve and Treasury authorities in the implementation of their policies. The specific measures of fluctuations examined included: (1) the net inflow of funds, (2) dividend rates paid on savings and loan accounts, (3) the volume of mortgage loans, (4) mortgage commitments, and (5) bond investments and liquid reserves.

The principal hypothesis employed is that if savings and loan operations are, in the main, sensitive to monetary policy measures, associations will react in countercyclical fashion as monetary policy actions are put in motion. On the other hand, if the movements of the variables listed above bear little or no relationship to the cycle, it can be concluded that associations are not significantly affected by monetary policy or that their operations are dominated by other forces.

In addition, this chapter will include a discussion of the applicability

109

of the Gurley-Shaw thesis to savings and loan associations. This thesis holds that federal monetary and debt management authorities are unable to exercise much power or control over the investment operations of savings and loan associations. It maintains that the control exerted by monetary authorities over commercial banking and the money supply is subject to considerable diminution as it passes into the area of non-monetary intermediaries. Accordingly, advocates of the theory imply that direct controls should be placed by government on the ability of savings and loan associations and other nonmonetary intermediaries to sell their liquid claims for money. Such suggestions are advanced in the interest of equalizing the alleged hardships placed on commercial banks in the competitive struggle with intermediaries, as well as to provide more efficient monetary management in the national interest. The most common control suggested is some type of a reserve requirement for savings and loan associations.

Monetary Policy and Savings Flow

Savings flows into savings and loan associations have displayed a strong secular forward thrust for over a generation. In every year since 1939, associations have taken into gross savings more dollars than they did in the previous year. Although withdrawals have also risen, the growth of gross inflows was sufficiently strong so that net savings receipts were progressively larger throughout almost the entire period. Since the end of World War II, only in 1948 and 1957 did net savings receipts dip below the gain reported for the previous year, and there was also a decrease in the number of new savings accounts opened at associations during those two years.

It is noteworthy that the two years in which savings gains slowed were the peak years immediately preceding the two most serious post-war recessions in this country. This illustrates very well the counter-cyclical character of savings flows into savings and loan associations.[1] It appears that savings flows into associations decrease and outflows rise as prosperity periods reach their climax. With consumer confidence high, it may be that the greater optimism existing at such times toward purchase of durables, down payments on homes, stock market investments, and other uses of liquid funds is responsible. On the other hand, if data on the later 1950's is indicative, savings tend to rise as consumers become convinced that the economic outlook has worsened. For example, after slowing through the first half of 1957, savings flow began to rise very strongly and continued its rise throughout 1958.

This can be seen in Chart 7-1, which also compares net savings at savings and loan associations with the course of monetary policy as

---

[1] This subject was discussed previously in Chapter 5.

depicted by the Federal Reserve discount rate at its New York Bank. Seasonally adjusted, net savings declined during 1956 and 1957 as monetary policy became more restrictive. Later, as money conditions eased, savings rose rapidly through 1958 and into 1959.

CHART 7-1

NET SAVINGS AT SAVINGS AND LOAN ASSOCIATIONS
AND FEDERAL RESERVE DISCOUNT RATE

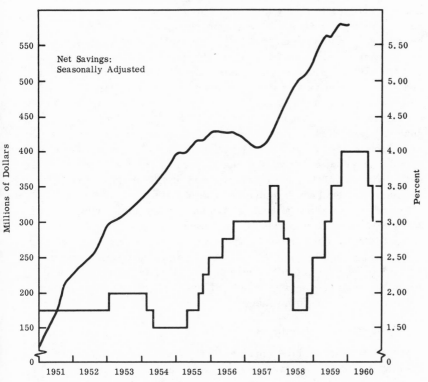

Source: Federal Reserve Board; net savings based on reports of the Federal Home Loan Bank Board.

To the extent that savings attitudes of the American consumer can be tied to monetary policy, it appears that savings at savings and loan associations perform as a sort of built-in stabilizer in our economy. Increased caution on the part of consumers causes a slowdown in withdrawals, net savings rise, and more funds made available to the construction industry, giving added incentive to that sector of American enterprise. Conversely, the slowing of savings flow in peak periods tends to decrease the supply of funds available for mortgages at precisely the time when the mortgage demand reaches its peak, and has the effect of pushing mortgage rates higher. The rise in the home financing charge serves to ration funds in this sector by eliminating the marginal borrower.

Monetary Policy and Loan Repayments

Monetary policy affects the cash flow of savings and loan associations through the influence it exerts on mortgage repayments. Mortgage repayments constitute a very important part of an association's gross cash flow.[2] The regular amortized payments on mortgages are not affected by monetary policy; but mortgage repayments, that is, unscheduled prepayments or the paying off of mortgages in whole or in part, are affected. When credit is eased and interest rates are declining, refinancing and repayments rise; to some degree, consumers tend to pay ahead on their mortgages at times when, in their eyes, the economic climate is becoming clouded. In periods of booming business activity, monetary restriction, and rising interest rates, the conditions for refinancing becomes less favorable and prepayments fall. Such a conclusion must be tempered by recognition that in periods of vigorous home building activity, complete loan payoffs rise due to sale of existing properties and affect money flows at individual institutions.

As indicated earlier, a savings and loan association seeing its cash flow declining tends to become more cautious about its forward commitments to builders and more concerned about its liquidity position. As a consequence, higher standards are placed on mortgage loans, and interest rates on new loans tend to move higher. These techniques are used to ration the relatively limited supply of available home financing funds at the disposal of the institution.

Monetary Policy and Dividend Rates

Monetary policy and debt management have a twofold relationship to the rate of return which savings and loan associations pay to their savers. On the one hand, during periods of increasingly tight monetary conditions and rising interest rates, associations find that the yield available to them from mortgages tends to rise and push association earnings to higher levels. Consequently, the rate of return they are able to pay to their savers also moves higher. It should be kept in mind, however, that because the mortgage portfolio has been built up over a period of many years, the increase in total earnings tends to build up much more slowly than the rise in current mortgage rates might indicate. For example, between 1954 and 1957, the typical mortgage rate on conventional loans moved upward from 5 percent to 6 percent, a good 20 percent gain. Dur-

---

[2] See Tables 5-3 and 6-2.

ing the same period, however, gross earnings on association mortgage portfolios rose from 4.91 percent to 5.11 percent, an increase of only 4 percent.

Savings and loan associations, as institutional investors, specialize in long-term assets. The average life of a mortgage loan is between six and seven years. This means that associations get a cash pay-back of only about 15 percent each year. If, on top of this money flow, we assume a growth rate of approximately 5 percent, associations come into the market each year with an amount totaling no more than 20 percent of their portfolio seeking reinvestment. Thus, they find themselves at a relative disadvantage during periods of tightening money conditions compared with an institution that has short-term assets that turn over in less than a year and that can capture the higher interest rates very quickly and run them through into its earnings. In order to cope with this problem, associations have tended to affix to loans fees and charges that can be taken into income during the year the loan is made. Borrowers seem more interested in the availability of funds than in the rate of interest, and a fee of 0.5 percent at the time the loan is made becomes a secondary consideration if the funds desired are available. This may be true partly because interest is deductible from taxable income.

Since 1949 the trend in savings and loan dividend payments has been steadily upward. The strongest increases occurred between 1956 and 1960, at the same time that money market rates reached their highest levels of the postwar period and monetary policy was restrictive.[3] Because associations for the most part follow the policy of announcing intended or anticipated rates of payments to savers at the beginning of semiannual dividend periods, the yields on savings and loan accounts as usually computed and published tend to lag behind market facts. They do not reflect as closely as they might the effects of monetary policy actions on dividend rates from the view of timing.

Associations must pay a dividend return at the specified rate to all savers, both new and old, and on all accounts, rather than simply on the marginal funds stimulated by any rate increase in the current period. The stimulus to move to a higher dividend rate stems from the desire to honor existing demands for mortgage funds and to support the home financing needs of the community at as high a level as possible. Managers usually conclude that it is better to pay the price required by the savings market to secure the funds for the potential home owner than to pass out of the lending picture.

Another way in which monetary policy affects the dividend rates offered to savers by savings and loan associations is through its effect on yields from competitive investments. As competition for funds increases

---

[3] See Tables 4-5 and 4-6.

due to restrictive monetary policy and the relatively short supply of funds as compared with the demand for them, all agencies seeking savings from individuals and others push the rate of return offered to savers to higher levels. Between 1950 and 1960 mutual savings banks increased the yield offered to savers by 1.6 percent; commercial banks increased the yield offered by 1.6 percent; yields on United States long-term bonds rose 1.7 percent, on municipal bonds 1.7 percent, and on corporate bonds 1.8 percent. During the same period, savings and loan associations increased the annual yield offered on their accounts by 1.2 percent. Thus, throughout the broad range of investment outlets available to individuals there was a striking similarity in the increase in yield offered. Differentials existing in 1950 continued to exist in 1959. Since 1950 a steadily increasing proportion of the gross income of savings and loans has been distributed among account holders as a return on their savings (Table 7-1).

TABLE 7-1
Percentage Distribution of Savings and Loan Associations
Gross Income
1949-1960

Year	Operating Expenses	Other Charges	Total to Expenses	Allocation to Reserves	Dividend to Savers	Total
1949	28.0%	1.8%	29.8%	22.7%	47.5%	100.0%
1950	27.1	2.1	29.2	24.8	46.0	100.0
1951	27.1	2.7	29.8	23.2	47.0	100.0
1952	27.0	2.8	29.8	21.0	49.2	100.0
1953	25.9	2.7	28.6	21.0	50.4	100.0
1954	25.3	2.2	27.5	21.3	51.2	100.0
1955	24.5	2.4	26.9	21.8	51.3	100.0
1956	24.2	2.7	26.9	20.3	52.8	100.0
1957	23.6	2.4	26.0	18.3	55.7	100.0
1958	23.1	1.9	25.0	18.4	56.6	100.0
1959	22.6	2.6	25.2	17.9	56.9	100.0
1960	22.3	2.3	24.6	17.5	57.9	100.0

Source: United States Savings and Loan League, based on data of Federal Home Loan Bank Board.

Monetary Policy and Mortgage Lending

The effect of monetary policy is most pronounced on the lending side of the savings and loan business. Chart 7-2 shows the relationship between mortgage lending at savings associations, seasonally adjusted, and the trend in the Federal Reserve discount rate at its New York Bank. The discount rate is used as a general measure of the degree of tightness in monetary policy. Notice that in 1955, 1956, and 1957, when monetary policy was firm, lending at associations did decline. In late 1957 and in 1958, easier money conditions were accompanied by a sharp upswing in mortgage lending activity. Late in 1959, as the last few points on the chart indicate, monetary policy served to slow the volume of mortgage lending. In the most recent downturn there appears to be a lag in the effect of tightening money conditions upon the savings and loan business. Monetary climate is only one of many factors influencing activity in the housing sector. It appears that the effects of financing terms on the housing market become less pronounced after 1960.

CHART 7-2
MORTGAGE LENDING AT SAVINGS AND LOAN ASSOCIATIONS
AND FEDERAL RESERVE DISCOUNT RATE

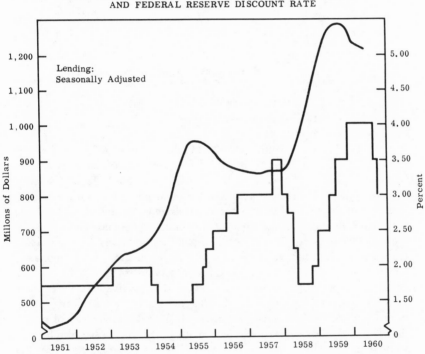

Source: Federal Reserve Board; mortgage lending based on reports of the Federal Savings and Loan Insurance Corporation.

Possibly more direct evidence of the extent of the lag in home building and mortgage lending appears in the record made in commitments and purchases during 1958 and 1959 by the Federal National Mortgage Association under its Special Assistance Program 10 (Table 7-2). This was the $1 billion of housing funds authorized by the Emergency Housing

TABLE 7-2
Commitments and Purchases by the Federal National Mortgage
Association under Its Special Assistance Program 10[1]

(Millions of Dollars)

Year and Quarter	Commitments[2]	Purchases
1958: 1st	---	---
2nd	$ 411.6	
3rd	578.2	$ 9.0
4th	10.2	92.5
1959: 1st	---	272.4
2nd	---	282.8
3rd	---	167.2
4th	---	17.4
1960: 1st	---	1.2
TOTAL	$1,000.0	$842.5

[1]One billion dollars, authorized by the Emergency Housing Act of 1958
for the purchase of FHA-insured and VA-guaranteed mortgages of
$13,500 or less.
[2]Commitments under Program 10 were made only in 1958.

Source: Federal National Mortgage Association.

Act of 1958. The funds were authorized in the spring of 1958 and the peak of commitments occurred in the third quarter of 1958—but the peak of purchases did not take place until the second quarter of 1959. The cycle of commitment, housing start, construction expenditure, and mortgage loan closing can extend over a period of six months or more. The speed with which monetary action affects home building depends on the time of the year—particularly the time of the home building year—that an action takes place. The lag, for example, would be greater if the monetary action took place in June or July than if it were to take place in December, January, or February. Builders and their financiers need time to develop their land holdings, designs, models, sales force, and so on, in order to respond to monetary actions. If a sizable inventory of unsold dwelling units existed, as is the case with lower unit cost durables, the story might be different. But this is not the case. Professor G. Walter Woodworth of the University of Illinois has pointed out that the relatively long life of a house as a durable and the importance of financing in the transaction put housing in a class by itself as far as monetary impact is concerned.[4]

Let us look more closely at actions based on monetary policy and note their effect, or lack of effect, on savings and loan operation in the most

---

[4] *1960 Proceedings Conference on Savings and Residential Financing* (Chicago: United States Savings and Loan League, 1960), pp. 57-80.

recent period of tight money. In 1959 and early 1960 the Federal Reserve System maintained a relatively high discount rate in the face of a strong demand for credit. Interest rates rose in the short-term market and mortgage loan rates reached a plateau not witnessed for years. The high rates of interest on contracts demanded by the lenders exerted a restrictive effect on housing starts and mortgage commitments and on the real estate and home building segment of the economy. By mid-1959 the effects could be observed on housing starts and on mortgage lending at associations.

Other effects of money tightness on associations in 1959 were these: (1) the rate on advances to its members from the Federal Home Loan Banks rose sharply in 1959 as the FHLB System passed on the higher price it paid for funds in the capital market; (2) competition for savings funds increased, especially from commercial banks, and rates of return offered to savers rose; (3) liquidity of associations was drawn down, intensifying the pressure on new lending and lending terms; (4) loan repayments, especially advance repayments of mortgages, tended to slow; (5) associations with sizable portfolios of long-term mortgage contracts written at lower interest rates found their earning power threatened by rising money costs.

In short, an effective tight money policy tends to curtail lending activity at associations, just as at banks. The precise timing, however, may vary.

Association managers, dealing as they do almost entirely in conventional loans, also feel some shift to their institutions of the mortgage demand which previously went into the government-backed sector of the market—FHA and VA mortgages—and to lenders specializing in these types of contracts. As monetary policy tightens, insurance companies and banks tend to move from government insured and guaranteed mortgages, where interest rates have rigid ceilings, to alternate investment opportunities. This move can increase the demand for mortgage funds in the conventional market at precisely the time when savings and loan associations are already feeling the effects of a somewhat reduced savings flow and a decline in repayments. As a consequence, the conventional sector of the market finds it more difficult to meet its demand and the workings of monetary policy begin to intensify, as desired.

Monetary and Debt Management Policy and Bond Investments

The holdings of United States government securities by savings and loan associations rose more than those of any other intermediary during the 1950's (Table 7-3), rising from $1.5 billion in 1950 to $4.6 billion in 1960. Life insurance companies and mutual savings banks, on the other hand, reduced relatively and absolutely their dollar holdings of such obligations. The main reasons for the growth in holdings by savings

118   Influence on Savings Flow and Investment Process

TABLE 7-3
United States Government Security Holdings
Of Major Institutions
(Millions of Dollars)

Institution	Assets 12-31-50	12-31-60	Percent Change	Government Securities 12-31-50	12-31-60	Percent Change
Commercial Banks	$168,932	$257,552	+ 52.5%	$ 62,027	$ 61,003	- 1.7%
Mutual Savings Banks	22,385	40,574	+ 81.3	10,868	6,239	- 42.6
Life Insurance Companies	64,020	119,717	+ 87.0	13,459	11,729	- 12.9
Savings and loan associations	16,893	71,489	+323.2	1,487	4,586	+208.4

Source: Federal Reserve Board.

associations have been their growth in assets and the liquidity requirements deemed necessary for associations by regulatory agencies and management.

Thus, the savings and loan business has become a sizable market for government obligations. In 1958, the Treasury recognized the status of savings associations as investors by requesting them to appoint and send to Washington upon the call of the Secretary of the Treasury a bond advisory committee similar to committees already in existence for commercial banks, insurance companies, and other institutional investors. Further evidence of their rising stature as buyers of government securities is the fact that in 1960 the Treasury instituted regular monthly surveys of holdings of governments by savings associations. Results of the surveys appear in the *Treasury Bulletin*.

Savings associations did not experience the locked-in effect during the 1950's as seriously as did other intermediaries. In the first place, the big liquidation in holdings of governments by savings associations had already taken place in 1946, 1947, and 1948. Association managers, by and large, considered the build-up of governments during the war years as a temporary expedient and were fully prepared to move out of governments into mortgages as soon as restrictions on home building and real estate activity were removed. The rapid liquidation was in line with the basic objective of associations—promoting home ownership on as broad a scale as possible. Although specific data on the composition of investment portfolios at associations during the 1940's do not exist, there is considerable informed opinion that a great proportion of their holdings was in the form of nonmarketable bonds. Such securities were readily redeemable at or close to par and were not subject to the sizable discounts that developed on marketable issues. Savings and loan managers, looking at their portfolio of nonmarketable bonds, such as Series F and G issues, could easily calculate the loss they would have to take and knew that it was limited. This specialized character of the holdings of government securities by savings associations, and the substantial growth in the assets of such institutions, kept to a minimum the pressure on bond portfolios as compared with that faced by other intermediaries holding government securities.

Secondly, growth in the savings and loan business was sufficiently strong in the 1950's so that holdings of governments did not have to be liquidated in order to secure funds for investments in other assets. Savings associations were able to take advantage of the higher yields being offered on securities floated by the federal government during the middle and later years of the decade.

Another way in which savings associations aid monetary management is through the purchase of government agency obligations. Associations have become a sizable factor in the market for FNMA notes and FHLB consolidated obligations, holding over $500 million or 13 percent of such obligations outstanding at the end of 1959. Because these holdings are not part of the legal liquidity requirements at savings associations, they represent a removal from the mortgage market of funds which could be used to meet demands in that area.

Through their government portfolio transactions, savings associations also tend to stabilize the rate on Treasury bills. They do this in the following way: When the rate on Treasury bills exceeds the rate on Federal Home Loan Bank time accounts, associations tend to move into the Treasury bill market, increasing the demand for bills and thereby tending to hold down this rate. At other times, when bill rates fall below the rate available on time accounts at Federal Home Loan Banks, associations may transfer funds from the bill market to their Federal Home Loan Bank accounts and thereby prevent the bill rate from falling as low as it otherwise might.

Use of Borrowed Funds

The seasonal deficiency in the normal flow of funds at savings associations relative to mortgage demand was demonstrated in Chapter 6. For the most part, that deficiency is met through borrowed money, secured primarily in the form of advances from the Federal Home Loan Banks. In a normal year, the most sizable increases in borrowings occur in the peak lending season—June through September. Associations also borrow to meet unanticipated cyclical upswings in the demand for mortgage funds. This latter type of borrowing is sometimes interpreted as being in conflict with monetary policy.

Savings associations using Federal Home Loan Bank funds feel directly the impact of monetary policy because the Home Loan Banks, through the mechanism of consolidated Federal Home Loan Bank System obligations, obtain the funds they lend to members from the money and capital markets of the nation. When the Federal Reserve, through its policies, curbs the supply of credit, the Federal Home Loan Banks find the cost of funds which they pass on to associations is higher (Table 7-4). The responsiveness of rate increases to monetary policy

TABLE 7-4
**Advance Rate at Federal Home Loan Bank of Chicago
and Federal Reserve Discount Rate - New York
1950–1961**

Year and Quarter	FHLB Advance Rate	FRB Discount Rate	Year and Quarter	FHLB Advance Rate	FRB Discount Rate
1950 - 1st	2.00%	1.50%	1956 - 1st	3.25%	2.50%
2nd	2.00	1.50	2nd	3.25	2.75
3rd	2.00	1.50-1.75	3rd	3.50	2.75-3.00
4th	2.00	1.75	4th	3.75	3.00
1951 - 1st	2.00	1.75	1957 - 1st	3.75	3.00
2nd	2.00	1.75	2nd	3.75	3.00
3rd	2.25	1.75	3rd	4.25	3.00-3.50
4th	2.25	1.75	4th	4.25	3.50-3.00
1952 - 1st	2.25	1.75	1958 - 1st	3.25	2.75-2.25
2nd	2.50	1.75	2nd	3.00	1.75
3rd	2.50	1.75	3rd	3.00	1.75-2.00
4th	2.50	1.75	4th	3.50	2.00-2.50
1953 - 1st	2.50	2.00	1959 - 1st	3.75	2.50-3.00
2nd	2.50	2.00	2nd	4.25	3.00-3.50
3rd	3.00	2.00	3rd	5.00	3.50-4.00
4th	3.00	2.00	4th	5.00	4.00
1954 - 1st	3.00	2.00-1.75	1960 - 1st	4.50	4.00
2nd	2.50	1.50	2nd	4.00	4.00-3.50
3rd	2.50	1.50	3rd	3.50	3.50-3.00
4th	2.50	1.50	4th	3.50	3.00
1955 - 1st	2.50	1.50	1961 - 1st	3.25	3.00
2nd	2.50	1.75-2.00-2.25	2nd	3.25	3.00
3rd	3.00	1.75			
4th	3.25	2.25-2.50			

Sources: Federal Home Loan Bank Board; Federal Reserve Board.

changes is intensified by the existence of an escalator clause in the notes used by most Federal Home Loan Banks. The clause makes the higher rate applicable to all outstanding advances as well as to new borrowing.

Thus, during periods of tight money and monetary restraint, associations must pay considerably higher prices for Federal Home Loan Bank funds, and exhibit reactions similar to those of a commercial banker viewing the Federal Reserve discount rate or a business borrower viewing the cost of borrowing on commercial paper. The year 1959 provides an outstanding illustration. On February 16, the Home Loan Bank System borrowed funds to make advances at a cost of 3.725 percent. Later issues were floated at successively higher rates and by October their borrowing cost was 5.5 percent. The lending rates on advances to savings associations rose accordingly. Thus, another effect of monetary policy on associations is that borrowing of marginal increments of funds from the Home Loan Banks becomes less and less attractive as restraint increases. Incentives to pay off advances heighten whenever escalator clauses push rates on existing borrowings higher. In addition, the presidents of the Federal Home Loan Banks have an obligation to employ moral suasion in determining the level of advances to the various member institutions seeking to borrow from them.

What at times appears to be a conflict between the policy of the Federal Reserve System and the policy of the Federal Home Bank Board regarding money matters arises by accident rather than by design. As noted earlier, considerable time elapses between the making of a mortgage commitment to a builder by a savings association and the taking down of that loan by a home buyer. Imperfect knowledge of money flows during the interval involved may make recourse to FHLB advances necessary, and any government agency would find it difficult to refuse the Home Loan Bank System the right to borrow at a time when it must borrow in order to make advances to associations for the fulfillment of loan commitments made months before. Ideally, the denial would have had to take place during the period when the advance commitments were made.

For example, assume that the Federal Reserve and the Treasury desired to limit advances through the Federal Home Loan Bank System during the 1959 upsurge in mortgage lending. The appropriate time for the restraint to be exercised was not in the fall of 1959 when it became apparent that commitments were unusually high, but rather in late 1957 and early 1958 when the commitments to builders were being made. It would have taken extremely farsighted individuals in government to have stated at that time that mortgage commitments would amass at an extremely rapid pace and that they should be curtailed, because a turn in the direction of economic activity was imminent. In such an instance, to rely on any individual or government agency rather than on market forces seems to overestimate the infallibility of such a person or agency. The lag between commitment and loan closing is a very real part of home finance.

Summary

The effects of monetary policy on savings and loan associations may be assessed in two ways: First, in terms of the direct effects of monetary restraint on associations and, second, in terms of the extent to which association operations work in harmony with and are responsive to the objectives of monetary policy.

As monetary restraint increases, the following pattern evolves:

1) Mortgage lending activity begins to slow. Loan rates rise, discouraging marginal builder and home buyer.

2) Rates of return on competitive investment media tend to rise, forcing savings associations to meet these increases.

3) Expectations regarding cash flows are cut back, commitments to builders and others for future loans are shortened, and commitment fees are raised.

4) Marginal increments of funds to support mortgage lending, such as FHLB advances, can be secured only by paying the full interest cost exacted by the monetary restraint in the capital markets. Escalator clauses broaden this impact.

The ability of savings associations to work in harmony with the objectives of monetary policy are indicated by the following:

1) Mortgage repayments and prepayments tend to slow, decreasing the pool of funds available to support new lending.

2) Monetary policy tends to shift demand for FHA and VA financing, normally handled by other lenders, into the conventional sector, placing greater pressure on savings associations for loans and increasing interest rates.

3) Since the term of their earning assets may range to a period of twenty years and beyond, savings associations find a sizable portion of their portfolio locked into yields which may be well below current yields. As a result, associations are unable fully to adjust their mortgage asset portfolio to the higher dividend rates offered on all savings accounts. The net result is a shrinkage of the margin between dividend pay-outs and gross income. Thus, the length of mortgage portfolios makes savings and loans less able to adjust to extended periods of restraint than other lenders.

Applicability of the Gurley-Shaw Thesis

The Gurley-Shaw thesis and its applicability to savings and loan associations and other intermediaries has been a very live topic. In essence, this theoretical argument for control of intermediaries is based on the concept of a "deposit rate" which allegedly permits nonmonetary intermediaries to attract funds and grow at a relatively faster pace than monetary agencies (banks) when governmental authorities restrict credit and interest rates rise. The rate of return on primary securities (bonds, mortgages, etc.) rises and, in theory, there is an increase in the spread between the price at which nonmonetary intermediaries sell their liquid claims for money (savings accounts) and the rates at which they lend. Spending units (individual consumers) are in turn encouraged to reduce their demand for money and accept holdings which are considered highly liquid substitutes. Thus, since the interest rate is higher than it would have been in the absence of the nonmonetary intermediaries, and the price level is higher, it is concluded that the action of savings associations and other intermediaries handicaps the effectiveness of a restrictive monetary policy. Because the monetary authorities have in mind a certain goal regarding tightness, they must press even more severely on commercial bank credit to achieve that goal and thus, the implication goes, adversely affect the commercial banks and their ability to grow.

The following excerpt presents the basic framework of a "deposit rate":

> The willingness of nonmonetary intermediaries to supply claims on themselves, in real terms, depends on the rate of interest on primary securities that they buy, on the deposit rate of nonmonetary indirect debt that they sell, on their variable expenses in managing assets and liabilities, and on the types of primary securities available to them. An increase in the rate of interest on primary securities increases their willingness to supply nonmonetary indirect assets. They will also tend to supply less claims on themselves when the composition of primary securities is unfavorable to their activities.[5]

Such a position neglects the realities of the savings and loan business. Savings associations cannot automatically trade on a widening gap between the price they must pay for savings funds placed with them and the yield they are able to secure from mortgage investments. In reality, the margin narrows rather than widens in times of monetary restraint. The margin between the cost of money and the return on that money narrowed throughout the 1950's. Thus, to state, as Gurley and Shaw do, that intermediaries can benefit by taking the initiative in increasing or decreasing their holdings of liquid assets of consumers and thus frustrate the efforts of monetary authorities, ignores the fact that the operating margins of institutions during the period of tight money has been declining rather than increasing or remaining constant. The underlying reason that the Gurley-Shaw hypothesis breaks down is that a savings association pays the higher dividend rate on *all* savings balances held by that institution (not just marginal investments), but obtains the benefits of higher mortgage rates on a relatively limited volume of its total asset holdings. In fact, it may be said that pressures to maintain savings balances by paying competitive rates tend to act against savings associations with a leverage effect and to reinforce the pressure of monetary policy.

In addition, there appears to be at work in mortgage holdings a type

---

[5] J. B. Gurley and E. S. Shaw, *Money in a Theory of Finance* (Washington: The Brookings Institution), pp. 204-205.

of "Gresham's law in reverse," whereby the lower interest rate mortgages tend to remain on the books of the association relatively longer than the higher interest rate mortgages. Borrowers holding mortgages written during high yield periods tend to prepay or repay their obligations much more readily than do individuals holding favorable contracts and to re-finance these obligations whenever the interest rate cycle turns around. Although a typical association may have made mortgage loans in 1959 at 6.25 percent plus a commission or charge, a major share of its earning assets may well be mortgages written at rates of 5 percent and perhaps even lower.

In the same vein, Gurley and Shaw state:

> Private nonmonetary intermediaries are further aided if the monetary system's deposit rates are set at low levels and if monetary policy is generally restrictive. For then, assuming nonneutrality of money, rising interest rates on primary securities induce the private intermediaries to raise their own deposit rates for the purpose of attracting additional demand for their products. The growth of these intermediaries is also favored by governmental insurance of their indirect debts, by such insurance of at least some of the primary securities they purchase, and by the absence of competition from governmental lending institutions.

> Many of these factors are likely to be present during an upswing in private economic activity when aggregate demand for current output threatens to be excessive at prevailing price levels and when the Policy Bureau (the Federal Reserve authorities) attempts to protect these levels.[6]

Another factor this thesis fails to take into account is that savings associations, by and large, are mutual type institutions not necessarily working to maximize returns to stockholders in any specific time period or having a specific stockholder obligation, implicit or otherwise, period after period. The psychological orientation of savings and loan management may well be very different from that which is assumed in the Gurley-Shaw hypothesis.

Savings associations are not subject to direct control by monetary authorities in the sense that authorities exercise direct control over the commercial banking system and the supply of reserves in banks. However, in a series of powerful indirect ways, savings and loans do come under the influence of monetary controls. By affecting interest rates, the monetary authorities can have an important influence on: (1) the supply of funds flowing into associations in the form of new savings and mortgage repayments; (2) the supply of funds flowing into the home mortgage market from other mortgage investors, and competitive patterns in the market in which associations must confine their activities; (3) the price which associations must pay for savings and for marginal increments

---

[6] *Ibid.*, p. 229.

of loanable funds in the form of Federal Home Loan Bank advances; (4) the ability of associations to sell liquid assets and to raise additional funds for home mortgage investments; and (5) the willingness of associations to enter into forward commitments for home mortgages.

The most common implication flowing from the Gurley-Shaw thesis regarding savings and loan associations involves the imposition of reserve requirements upon these institutions. The alleged purpose of the measure is to give monetary authorities a means whereby they can control the lending ability of associations. Let us examine the suggestion that the liquid reserve of savings associations should be increased and made a required reserve similar to that maintained by commercial banks.

Reserve Requirements for Savings and Loans?

The primary function of the reserves required at commercial banks is not to provide safety or to assure availability of funds to depositors. Those responsibilities fall largely to bank management and its wisdom in the choice and distribution of earning assets, and to provisions of the insuring agencies. Nor is the reserve maintained as a reservoir which can be tapped to satisfy depositors' demands for cash withdrawals. In spite of the fact that minimum commercial reserve balances are held in the form of vault cash and balances in Federal Reserve Banks, they may not be used wholly to meet deposit withdrawals. In fact, they are relatively non-liquid assets maintained to assist monetary authorities to regulate the volume and the availability of commercial bank credit.

Credit restriction imposed by outside authority is not, however, particularly necessary in the case of savings associations. These institutions do not grant loans that build up deposit balances of borrowers, as is done by commercial banks. Nor do the savings accounts at associations circulate in the manner common to the deposits at commercial banks. The credit creation that is so essential to the successful operation of the commercial banking system is not a function of savings associations. And the restrictions imposed on the ability of commercial banks to add to the supply of purchasing power are not necessarily applicable to institutions that do not create deposits via their lending operations.

The liquidity of savings associations, as measured by cash, bank balances, and holdings of marketable government securities now exceeds 10 percent or more than double the legal reserve held against time and savings accounts at commercial banks. A savings association which receives funds from savers often limits its credit advances to somewhat less than the amount received. If the existing reserve is less than sufficient to cover the new account adequately, a portion of the receipts is retained as cash in its vault or is invested in legal securities. However, since most associations keep well over the legal minimum, the entire amount received may be used to enlarge the mortgage portfolio or other assets. In this respect, the operation of the thrift institution is similar to that of the individual commercial bank.

Determining Loanable Funds

The basis on which loans or credit advances are made by any financial institution is its "excess" reserve. This is the amount above the "legal" reserve, and may be termed "loanable funds." Ordinarily, when a customer of a commercial bank borrows, the proceeds of the loan are placed in his deposit account and some of the bank's excess reserve is shifted out of the excess category and becomes part of the legal minimum requirement.

Bank borrowers seldom request loans in excess of their needs, nor will they borrow before the need arises. Almost at once, therefore, the borrower will begin to check against his new deposit, and the lending bank may expect to lose reserves. Funds lost by one bank tend to flow into other banks within the system. The result is that each recipient of funds from the original lending bank now finds its deposits, reserves, and excess reserves expanded. Thus, banks with recently acquired excess reserves have a new and enlarged basis for lending or investing and, in the interests of their customers and themselves, seek to expand their loans and investments. As this process continues, it is evident that the primary deposit placed in the first bank has made possible a multiple expansion of deposits of "checkbook" money within the banking system.

A similar expansion does not occur among savings associations or other thrift institutions when loans are made by individual institutions. For every dollar it lends out, a savings association must secure a dollar from a saver or from another source. It trades one asset, dollars, for another, a mortgage. It does not create an asset by offering a liability. The proceeds of a loan are never used to create new savings accounts.

Focus of Control: Excess Funds

It is important to note that excess funds are substantially within the commercial banking system. The idle funds of an insurance company, for example, are represented typically by a deposit with a commercial bank, as are the idle funds of any corporation and, to some degree, the idle funds of a savings association. Thus, since the commercial bank plays the peculiar role of holding the cash balances of all other institutions, the focus of control in our monetary and economic system should properly be the commercial bank rather than the whole range of financial intermediaries. From the point of view of efficiency, control of monetary matters should be at the locus of idle funds rather than based on a broad approach of the type which the Gurley-Shaw thesis deems advisable. The generalizations incorporated in the hypothesis advocated by Gurley and

Shaw tend to oversimplify, and fail to take cognizance of the inner working of the savings and loan business.

A reserve requirement on savings associations through which their lending activities might be regulated would be somewhat comparable to the reserve requirement on time deposits at commercial banks which, at the present time, is at the level of 5 percent. Interestingly, the Federal Reserve System has adjusted or altered this percentage only once during the past eleven years: between January 1951 and June 1954 the requirement was moved to 6 percent. Apparently, Federal Reserve officials view the reserve requirement on time deposits as a device of limited importance in its kit of monetary control tools. A person advocating the establishment of reserve requirements on savings associations either would have to show that savings and loan accounts have characteristics more in common with demand deposits than with time deposits, or would be forced to indict the Federal Reserve System for its recent failures to deal aggressively with time deposit holdings of commercial banks in terms of monetary policy. Apparently our monetary authority feels that any transfers from demand deposits to time deposits have little telling effect on their ability to control the monetary system.

Direct control over savings associations by the monetary authorities is difficult to justify. The lending activities of associations are already substantially affected by policies of monetary authorities. The ultimate result of any direct controls might well be to thwart opportunities for further expanding the liquid savings of the American people and for providing economical home financing to American families. Both of these objectives are high on the list of public policy goals of our nation.

Government Housing Policy and Savings Flow and Investments

Monetary policy has had a unique impact on residential construction during the postwar years. Since the end of World War II a marked countercyclical tendency has been evident in the relation between residential construction and general business conditions. Housing starts moved sideways or downward during the prosperous periods—1951-53, 1956-57, and 1959-60—and rose quite sharply during the recession years—1954 and 1958.

One explanation of this volatile record of housing is the availability of mortgage financing. The cyclical instability has centered principally in FHA and VA construction. Conventionally financed starts, in which savings and loan associations specialize, have shown relative stability, in part because of shifts by some qualified home buyers from federally underwritten mortgages to conventional loans. The net result is that home building is said to have exerted a stabilizing influence on the economy as a whole.

Effect of Fixed Interest Rates on Housing Demand

Important institutional lenders shift between the FHA and VA mortgage market and competitive forms of investments as the yields on mortgages with fixed interest rates and other obligations change. When the yield differential between corporate bonds and FHA and VA mortgages rises, the number of housing starts usually declines, as in 1951-53, 1956-57, and 1959-60. On the other hand, when corporate rates decline in relation to federally underwritten mortgage rates, starts usually rise. The recession years—1954 and 1958—are cases in point. The wider fluctuation in VA starts as compared with FHA starts stems from the fact that the differential between yields on alternate investments and on VA home mortgages was greater than on those of the FHA.

Sharp cyclical swings occurred in the 1950's even though the practice of discounting federally underwritten mortgages rose to some prominence. Apparently, the discounting failed to substitute for free rates to the degree that the market desired, for it failed to stop transfers out of mortgages into other obligations. Until April 1958, the amount of the discount was limited by government regulations. In addition, both lenders and borrowers disliked to deal with each other on the basis of discounts from face value. It must be admitted, however, that if it had not been for discounting, volatility in the volume of FHA and VA financing might well have been greater than the records show.

On balance, it seems safe to say that monetary policy alternating from tightness to ease, when combined with fixed ceiling rates on government-backed mortgages, played a dominant role in year-to-year volatility of home building during the 1950's. Although it can be shown that the existence of interest rate ceilings on mortgages contributed significantly to the effectiveness of monetary policy in the housing area, such ceilings are by no means *essential* to the effectiveness of monetary policy on housing. As demonstrated earlier, monetary restraint does have an effect on conventional lending. The existence of ceilings tends to bunch demand and can lead to high cost, inefficient construction, and to increases in wage rates and material costs. Uneven utilization of resources raises demands for federal aid to the construction industry whenever volume declines and there is pressure upon marginal producers. When authorities seek to stimulate demand for funds during times of monetary ease, fixed interest rates can once again have an accelerating effect.

Longer View of Finance in Housing

Upward shifts in the maturity and down payment, as well as in interest rates, specified in both FHA and VA mortgage contracts, occurred during the 1950's, at precisely the time money market conditions eased and tended to accelerate the effective demand for houses by placing home-buying potential in the hands of greater numbers of families. The conventional loan was extended in a similar fashion. The liberalization of mortgage terms during the 1950's moved to a point, however, where further extension produced relatively little reduction in the monthly payment required of the typical home buyer. Unless new techniques of financing are instituted in the 1960's, shifts in the demand curve to include more income groups will have limited influence on housing volume.

During the years ahead, the cost and availability of mortgage credit may not be so vital a factor in the residential construction cycle. The postwar period to 1959 may have been unique in its strong, sustained demand for new houses. Throughout the 1950's, confidence in the long-run future was at a high level and consumers were willing to buy homes whenever mortgage funds were readily available and the terms eased. Factors other than financing which affect the housing cycle—the level of current income, the rate of household formation and family size, building costs, liquid asset holdings of potential homebuyers, etc.—may become relatively more important than they have been in the past.

Influence of Government Programs on Associations

What has this to do with the savings and loan business? As pointed out earlier, savings and loan associations made relatively little use of the FHA and VA home lending programs during the 1950's. Nevertheless, as the principal lender in the mortgage markets of the country, they found the guaranteed and insured programs of the federal government a prime competitor, with significant indirect effect on their own operations.

The liberal terms of government-assisted mortgage contracts undoubtedly led savings associations to push terms on conventional loans toward their legal maximums. For example, in 1951 their typical conventional mortgage called for a 37 percent down payment and a maturity of approximately sixteen years; by 1955, they had eased the terms to a down payment of 33 percent and a maturity of eighteen years; and in 1960, they were making conventional loans on a down payment of 26 percent and for maturities of twenty years and over (Table 7-5).

Another important indirect effect of FHA and VA ceilings is the way they concentrate loan demand at savings associations during periods when the FHA and VA programs suddenly become unattractive to other mortgage lenders. As lending rates on corporate securities and other investments available to insurance companies and mutual savings banks become relatively more attractive than those on government-assisted mortgages, these institutions switch funds from mortgages to corporates. As a consequence, savings associations suddenly find that the demand placed upon them for mortgage funds is growing. Cyclical peaks in FHLB advances to associations have occurred at precisely the times when the FHA and VA programs seemed to have lost their attractiveness.

TABLE 7-5
Trend in Terms of Conventional Mortgage Loans
At Savings and Loan Associations
on
$15,000 New House[1]
1954–1961

Year	Typical Ratio Loan To Purchase Price	Typical Interest Rate	Typical Maturity	Typical Monthly Payment
1954	65 - 70% (65%)	5%	15-17 yrs (17)	$71.08
1955	65 - 70% (66%)	5%	17-20 ($17\frac{1}{2}$)	70.69
1956	65 - 70% (67%)	$5\frac{1}{2}$%	17-20 (18)	73.47
1957	65 - 70% (68%)	6%	17-20 (19)	75.17
1958	70 - 75% (72%)	6%	17-20 ($19\frac{1}{2}$)	78.41
1959	70 - 75% (73%)	6%	20-25 (22)	74.90
1960	70 - 75% (74%)	6 - $6\frac{1}{4}$%	20-25 (23)	74.26
1961	70 - 75% (75%)	6 - $6\frac{1}{4}$%	20-25 (23)	75.26

[1]Assumes no inflation or construction cost increases.

Source: United States Savings and Loan League. Based on Survey Reports from 671 Associations in 1954 and over 1000 Associations in other years.

The liberalization of mortgage terms has been so strong that it might be typed as a secular shift. Pressures from builders and others for more liberal terms, following the lead introduced by FHA and VA transactions, intensified throughout the 1950's. Any cyclical tightening of terms did not endure long, for revival of the easing trend soon took place.

Summary

The existence of fixed rates on government insured and guaranteed mortgages has worked to accentuate the effects of monetary policy on the home mortgage market. They have inevitably placed great pressure on government to see that credit is available to the VA and FHA markets at a specified, often sub-market rate. Attempts to do this have included the expansion of FNMA purchases, direct loans, or the use of federal insurance funds to purchase government-assisted mortgages. Too often the use of such expediencies has run at cross purposes with Federal Reserve actions and has weakened the orderly influence of monetary policy on the housing sector. There is cause to believe that free mortgage market rates would produce a stable and more responsive mortgage and home building market. Housing activity during the years ahead may well be tied less to financial terms than it was during the 1950's.

Selective Credit Controls

The major selective credit control affecting savings and loan associations has been Regulation X, which went into effect in the autumn of 1950 as part of the Defense Production Act of that year and remained in operation until mid-1952. The regulation was designed to govern the expansion of residential mortgage credit terms and thus the level of home building. By controlling the amount of down payment and the length of time over which a mortgage could be written, it was hoped that the movement into home building of resources essential to the American defense effort could be controlled.

The impact in the conventional loan area, however, was less than might have been expected. Although housing starts in 1951 and 1952 were substantially lower than in 1950, the bulk of the decline took place in the FHA and VA sectors of the market. In 1951, FHA and VA starts combined were 40 percent below their 1950 level, while conventional housing starts were only 8 percent below the 1950 level. Part of the explanation rests in the manner in which the regulation was placed in effect. During the interval when authorities were required by law to consult with industrial groups in drafting these regulations, a large volume of commitments to provide financing at pre-Regulation X terms was built up by all types of mortgage lenders; and these commitments were, by and large, exempt from the regulation when it went into effect. Because of this backlog of mortgage commitments, along with the complexities of drafting rules covering the functioning of the mortgage market, the restrictive effects of Regulation X were considerably delayed.

Even more important, as far as the market effect of Regulation X on association lending was concerned, was the fact that restrictions on conventional loans and FHA-insured loans were identical and restrictions on VA-guaranteed loans were only slightly more liberal. For example, the maximum permissible loan amount on a $20,000 property was $11,700, or less than 60 percent of the value of the property; loans were limited to a maximum term of twenty years; and minimum amortization provisions were specified (on a $15,000 loan, the maximum advance was $10,700, or a little over 70 percent of the property value). Such terms were just about the same for the government-backed and conventional mortgages. They represented a more severe restriction on FHA and VA than on conventional lending. For the first time the conventional lender could compete with the FHA and VA lender on contract terms, for the typical loan at associations was then being written for fifteen to seventeen years with a 30 percent to 35 percent down payment. In fact, from the competitive point of view, association executives privately found much merit in the controls under Regulation X. This is not to say that associations seek or favor such administrative codes, but a shift of part of the housing demand from the more liberal government-assisted mortgage market to their institutions gave them entry into some markets for the first time.

Chapter 8

EARNING POWER

Although the term "earning power" is not commonly used by savings and loan executives, the concepts embodied in the phrase are a real part of the daily operations of savings associations. Trends in expense ratios, dividends and earnings, reserves and liquidity, and the future course of these measures, weigh heavily on management decisions. Broadly speaking, association management did a highly creditable job of improving the earning power of its institutions during the 1950's under conditions which were not always ideal. Management was forced to master the complex task of "digesting growth on the run" while frequently having to balance earnings on a long-term investment portfolio against a short-term, sharply rising cost of money. It was also called on to provide for the building of reserves and liquidity positions in line with the evolving character of the risks in the earning assets of the institution. Postwar trends in expenses, dividends, reserves, and liquidity are reviewed on the following pages.

Operating Expense and Gross Income

Expense Ratio

One of the best measures of how efficiently a business is being run on a year-to-year basis is the ratio of operating expense to gross income. This ratio, commonly called the operating ratio includes in its make-up all income accounts, operating and nonoperating, but for savings and loan associations it does not include interest on borrowed money, federal income tax, nonoperating charges, or dividends. A glance at Chart 8-1 shows that the trend in operating costs was one of improvement for savings associations throughout the postwar years. The ratio of operating expense to gross operating income declined steadily from almost 30 percent of gross income in 1946 to an estimated 23 percent at the end of 1959.

The ratio is dependent upon two variables: cost of operations and gross income. In order to determine the importance of these variables in the total picture, each was related to average assets for the period covered. Table 8-1 shows that between 1950 and 1960 gross income as a percentage of average assets increased from 4.45 percent to 5.53 percent, while operating expense decreased from 1.34 percent to 1.21 percent. The most striking improvements in the ratios occurred in 1954 and 1959, two years when net operating income as a percentage of average assets rose sharply. Thus, it seems that during the 1950's the increase in gross income was more important in producing a favorable operating ratio than was the decrease in operating expenses.

CHART 8-1

RATIOS OF OPERATING EXPENSE TO GROSS OPERATING INCOME
FOR ALL MEMBER ASSOCIATIONS OF THE FHLB SYSTEM, 1946 - 1960

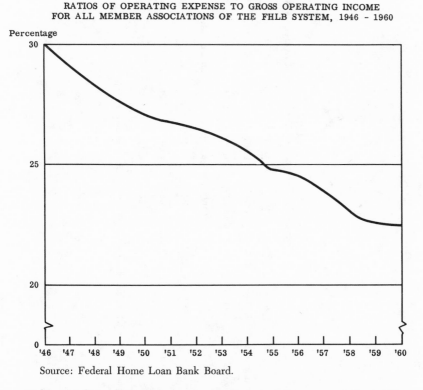

Source: Federal Home Loan Bank Board.

Table 8-2 lists the major expense items at savings associations. The most important operating expense is compensation, which takes about half of each expense dollar. While the trend in the relative share of expense dollars going to wages and salaries was downward during the 1950's, it is interesting to note that the greatest strides were made in this

TABLE 8-1

Income and Expense as a Percentage of Average Assets

	1950	1951	1952	1953	1954	1955	1956	1957	1958	1959	1960
Gross operating income	4.45%	4.49%	4.54%	4.50%	4.78%	4.87%	4.94%	5.09%	5.17%	5.35%	5.53%
Operating expense	1.34	1.34	1.31	1.32	1.33	1.25	1.28	1.26	1.24	1.19	1.21
Net operating income	3.11	3.15	3.23	3.18	3.45	3.62	3.66	3.83	3.93	4.16	4.32

Yearly Change of Income and Expense Ratios

	1950	1951	1952	1953	1954	1955	1956	1957	1958	1959	1960
Gross operating income	----	+.04	+.05	+.06	+.28	+.09	+.07	+.15	+.08	+.18	+.18
Operating expense	----	.00	-.03	+.01	+.01	-.08	+.03	-.02	-.02	-.05	+.02
Net operating income	----	+.04	+.08	+.05	+.27	+.17	+.04	+.17	+.10	+.23	+.16

Source: Based on more than 1,700 reports to the United States Savings and Loan League.

TABLE 8-2
Percentage Distribution of Total Operating Expense
1950–1959

	1950	1951	1952	1953	1954	1955	1956	1957	1958	1959[1]
Compensation	51.3%	51.2%	50.5%	50.6%	50.1%	49.8%	49.8%	48.2%	47.5%	46.8%
Cost of office space net[2]	5.2	5.2	5.2	5.2	5.4	5.4	5.6	5.8	6.1	6.4
Advertising	9.4	10.0	10.5	10.7	10.5	10.8	11.8	12.0	11.4	12.5
Federal insurance premium	4.7	4.8	5.3	5.3	5.4	5.5	5.7	5.8	5.8	5.8
Audit	0.8	0.7	0.6	0.8	0.7	0.8	0.8	0.8	0.8	0.8
Supervisory exams and assessments	1.4	1.2	1.3	1.2	1.2	1.1	1.2	1.2	1.3	1.3
Other operating expenses	27.2	26.9	26.6	26.2	26.7	26.6	26.0	26.2	27.1	26.4
Total	100.0%	100.0%	100.0%	100.0%	100.0%	100.0%	100.0%	100.0%	100.0%	100.0%

[1]Estimated.
[2]Expense items, "Rent, Light, Heat, etc." plus "Office Building Maintenance, Taxes, and Depreciation" less "Gross Income from Office Building."

Source: Based on data of all association members of FHLB System.

area only recently, since 1956, when savings and loan management became more actively interested in labor-saving devices and the placing of routine operations on a mechanical rather than hand-labor basis. Managers attribute the decrease in operating expenses to efficiency in manpower management through better training, departmentalization, mechanization of routine processes, and an improved work flow for the handling of day-to-day transactions.

One expense item which has been rising as a relative share of total expenses is advertising. In 1950, advertising took 9.4 percent of each operating expense dollar, while in 1959 it took 12.5 percent, an all-time high. Most other expenses have changed relatively little.

Does the size of an association or the population of the city in which it is located have any effect on its operating expenses? Generally, no. Although reports submitted to the United States Savings and Loan League reveal significant variations in the operating ratios of associations, the variations cannot be attributed to the size of the institution. Table 8-3 shows that, except at the very smallest institutions—those with assets of less than $2.5 million—operating ratios at associations are quite similar. Apparently economies of scale are not so readily available to mortgage lending institutions dealing in essentially local markets. The growth of automation may favor larger firms. That the size of the community in which an association is located does not greatly affect the operating expense ratio of associations, is shown in Table 8-4. Competitive influences may well raise expenses in the largest cities as associations seek to match one another in services rendered to customers, but the differences are not revealed as significant by the figures.

Approximately one-third of the reporting associations had an operating expense of less than 20 percent of gross income, another third

TABLE 8-3
**Percentage of Operating Expense to Total Gross Operating Income,
All Associations, by Asset Size Groupings
1957–1959**

Size of Association (Assets in Millions)	Percentage of Operating Expense to Gross Operating Income		
	1957	1958	1959
Under $2.5	25.7%	24.9%	26.7%
$2.5 and under $5	23.1	22.2	23.4
$5 and under $10	23.5	22.6	22.6
$10 and under $25	23.4	22.5	22.3
$25 and under $50	24.1	23.2	22.8
$50 and under $100	24.7	23.9	23.6
$100 and over	23.8	23.0	21.7
All groups	23.9	23.0	22.7

Sources: Federal Home Loan Bank Board; United States Savings and Loan League.

TABLE 8-4
Percentage Distribution of Associations with Respect
To Operating Expense Ratio and on Basis of
Population of City
1958

Percentage of Operating Expense to Gross Operating Income	Number of Associations	Percentage of Total Reporting	Percentage Distribution By Population of City		
			Under 100,000	100,000- 1,000,000	1,000,000 and over
Under 15%	111	7.7%	8.0%	6.2%	0.0%
15% and under 20%	358	24.7	25.6	17.2	21.6
20% and under 25%	498	34.4	31.9	35.3	28.4
25% and under 30%	253	17.5	20.8	24.8	32.8
30% and under 35%	150	10.4	9.4	9.7	12.7
35% and over	77	5.3	4.3	6.8	4.5
Total	1,447	100.0%	100.0%	100.0%	100.0%

Source: Based on 1,447 reports to the United States Savings and Loan League.

reported ratios of 20 percent to 25 percent, and the remaining third reported expense ratios in excess of 25 percent. Some of the factors responsible for the variations in operating ratios are these: (1) the number of services offered to customers; (2) differences in the degree of efficiency in handling transactions; (3) the number of separate offices maintained by an institution; (4) temporary overstaffing due to anticipation of rapid growth or other major changes in the near future; (5) the proportion of relatively low-yielding loans among earning assets, primarily VA and FHA loans; and (6) the proportion of funds held in the form of lower-earning liquid assets.

Sources of Gross Income

Table 8-5 indicates the relative importance of the various sources of gross income at savings associations. As would be expected, the bulk of the earnings comes from interest on mortgage loans and real estate contracts. With over 80 percent of assets invested in mortgage loans, one would expect that over 80 percent of gross income would come from this source. Throughout the 1950's, between 83 percent and 85 percent of gross income came from mortgage interest. Another income item of growing importance is premiums, commissions, and fees on mortgage loans, all of which are usually collected at the time a mortgage loan is closed. Their importance in gross income has risen over the past decade, and they now contribute approximately 8.5 percent of gross income. Cyclically the income derived from premiums, commissions, and fees appears to be the most volatile item in association receipts. During years in which real estate activity falls off, such as 1951 and 1956, associations are able to generate less income in this way.

TABLE 8-5
Sources of Gross Income of All Savings and Loan Associations
1941–1960

Year	Interest on Mortgage Loans	Interest on Other Investments	Premiums Commissions and Fees	Other Income	Total
1941	89.7%	1.0%	3.2%	6.1%	100.0%
1942	91.0	1.1	2.3	5.6	100.0
1943	88.6	3.2	2.6	5.6	100.0
1944	84.9	7.2	2.6	5.3	100.0
1945	77.9	11.0	2.5	8.6	100.0
1946	76.5	12.0	2.7	8.8	100.0
1947	82.8	9.2	2.9	5.1	100.0
1948	86.2	7.1	3.2	3.5	100.0
1949	86.1	6.1	4.0	3.8	100.0
1950	85.1	5.3	5.9	3.7	100.0
1951	86.1	5.0	4.9	4.0	100.0
1952	85.4	4.9	5.4	4.3	100.0
1953	84.6	4.8	6.1	4.5	100.0
1954	84.3	4.5	6.6	4.6	100.0
1955	84.3	4.1	7.4	4.2	100.0
1956	84.7	4.3	7.1	3.9	100.0
1957	83.9	4.6	7.5	4.0	100.0
1958	83.3	4.7	7.6	4.4	100.0
1959	82.7	5.0	8.3	4.0	100.0
1960 p	82.3	5.1	8.5	4.1	100.0

p – Preliminary.

Source: United States Savings and Loan League, based on data of Federal Home Loan Bank Board.

Dividends and Earnings

"Net income" at savings and loan associations is the residual after expenses of operation and interest payments on borrowed money have been met, and after nonoperating income and charges have been accounted for. Analysis of Table 8-6 reveals one outstanding fact: The saver fared well at the hand of savings associations during the postwar years. The share of income going to savers in the form of dividends rose persistently throughout the period. In 1950, association savers received 65 percent of net income (46 percent of gross income) as dividends; in 1960 the returns paid to savers took nearly 77 percent of net income (57 percent of gross income). In 1960, $2.0 billion was paid to association savers; this was more than double the amount paid in 1955 and more than six times the amount paid in 1950. Thus, the outstanding beneficiary of savings and loans' earning power during the 1950's was the saver.

Reserves and Liquidity

Throughout the years one of the major objectives of savings and loan management has been the steady build-up of reserve accounts for the sake of safety. Reserves are designed to absorb any losses incurred during the life of the risk assets and, by channeling earnings year after year into designated reserve accounts, associations prepare themselves to absorb any potential losses which may be realized. The build-up of reserves between 1946 and 1960 is shown in Table 8-7. Although the dollar additions to reserves mounted rapidly throughout the period, the reserve ratio (i.e., the ratio of reserves, surplus, and undivided profits to

TABLE 8-6
Allocation of Savings and Loan Association Net Income to Dividends and Reserves
All Associations

Year	To Dividends	To Reserves	Year	To Dividends	To Reserves
1945	66.5%	33.5%	1953	70.7%	29.3%
1946	63.6	36.4	1954	70.7	29.3
1947	66.2	33.8	1955	70.2	29.8
1948	67.4	32.6	1956	72.3	27.7
1949	67.7	32.3	1957	75.3	24.7
1950	65.0	35.0	1958	75.5	24.5
1951	67.0	33.0	1959	76.1	23.9
1952	70.0	30.0	1960 p	76.6	23.4

p - Preliminary.

Source: United States Savings and Loan League, based on data of Federal Home Loan Bank Board.

TABLE 8-7
Net Additions to and Total Reserves[1] of
All Savings and Loan Associations
1946–1960

Year	Net Addition to Reserves		Total Reserves	
	Millions of Dollars	Percentage of Gross Income	Millions of Dollars	Percentage of Total Savings
1946	$107	25.5%	$ 751	8.79%
1947	104	23.4	855	8.77
1948	114	22.5	969	8.84
1949	137	22.7	1,106	8.87
1950	174	24.8	1,280	9.15
1951	173	23.2	1,453	9.02
1952	205	21.0	1,658	8.64
1953	237	21.0	1,895	8.31
1954	285	21.3	2,180	8.03
1955	354	21.8	2,534	7.90
1956	378	20.3	2,912	7.85
1957	409	18.3	3,321	7.93
1958	475	18.4	3,796	7.93
1959	597	19.4	4,393	8.05
1960	589	17.5	4,982	8.02

[1]Includes reserves, undivided profits, and surplus.

Source: Based on data of the Federal Home Loan Bank Board.

savings capital) remained fairly steady. Thus, reserve accumulations kept pace with the expansion of the business. Associations are presently allocating to reserves approximately 18 percent of their income after operating expenses. A period of slower asset growth would see reserve ratios rise strongly. At the close of 1959, based on reports from a large, representative group of associations, 64 percent showed a reserve of between 6 percent and 10 percent of total assets; one in every fifteen reported a reserve of 10 percent or more; approximately 29 percent had a reserve position of less than 6 percent.

The liquidity of savings and loan associations was reviewed at some length in Chapters 5 and 6. Here let us simply restate that the typical savings association carries almost double the new legal requirement of 7 percent (effective January 1, 1961) of total savings. Determined by management, the liquidity position at a specific association is based on its needs to meet cash demands.

Associations also can secure liquid funds through their membership in the Federal Home Loan Bank System. Each institution has a line of credit determined by its regional Bank which, at present, may run up to 17.5 percent of savings capital. These factors, when combined with the considerable degree of built-in liquidity at associations, make the savings and loan business of today considerably more liquid than at any time in the past. Not only can associations expect monthly amortized mortgage payments to supply a steady inflow of funds, but they can also sell mortgages. Government-underwritten mortgages can be sold in the secondary market, and conventional loan participations can be sold to other associations under the Participation Loan Program authorized by the Federal Home Loan Bank Board.

Summary

Savings and loan associations have performed a creditable task in reducing their cost of operations at a time when inflationary pressures and rising wage rates were making this a most difficult task. Through various economies and efficiencies, operating expenses were reduced 23 percent between 1950 and 1959. There seems to be some variation in expense ratios at different size associations, caused primarily by differences in services rendered. During the years ahead, competition among associations may well become more intense; if it does, the earnings squeeze can but serve to heighten pressures for further improvements in operating efficiency.

Chapter 9

THE DEPRESSION EXPERIENCE

Causes of the Difficulties

Historians and economists commonly attribute many of the difficulties of the 1930's to the excesses of the 1920's. This can also be applied to the savings and loan business. The assets of the business climbed from $2.5 billion at year-end 1920 to $8.7 billion at year-end 1929, and the number of associations increased from 8,633 to 12,342. Many did not weather the hard times which were to follow.

In the years following the stock market crash in 1929, confidence in the future of business activity declined, unemployment increased, payrolls decreased, financial institutions failed, and the value of the asset of investors fell substantially. All of this had serious repercussions on the savings and loan business. Heavy demands for withdrawals were made upon associations, not only because of a decline in confidence in financial and other business institutions, but also because of the increased need on the part of investors to draw on savings to augment currently declining incomes.

The business situation was made more difficult in many instances by the collapse of the commercial banking system. The deposits of savings associations were frozen in closed banks and many borrowers were unable to draw on their checking accounts to meet their loan repayments. In virtually every area in which a savings association failed or was closed, one or more commercial banks in that area had closed previously. By the same token, it is generally true that in areas where the commercial banks remained open, most, if not all, of the savings associations also remained open.

Losses Suffered by Associations

During the 1930's, 1,706 associations failed, with estimated losses to savers of approximately $200 million. The year-by-year record is shown in Table 9-1. However, losses in the savings and loan business were not restricted to the associations which failed. Many associations which remained open also suffered considerable losses on their mortgage portfolios.

Until recently there had never been an adequate study of depression losses in the savings and loan business. The only clues to depression losses

TABLE 9-1
Savings and Loan Association Failures
1930–1939
(In Thousands of Dollars)

Year Ending December 31	Number of Assns. Failing	Total Liability of Failed Assns.	Percentage of Liability of Failed Assns. to Liability of All Assns.	Estimated Losses to Shareholders	Percentage of Losses to Total Assets of All Associations
1930	190	$ 80,430	0.93%	$24,676	0.2795%
1931	126	61,909	0.70	22,328	0.2653
1932	122	52,818	0.63	20,337	0.2624
1933	88	215,517	2.78	43,955	0.6299
1934	68	34,728	0.50	10,174	0.1577
1935	239	31,946	0.50	15,782	0.2680
1936	144	20,316	0.34	9,052	0.1576
1937	269	44,739	0.78	15,775	0.2761
1938	277	36,025	0.64	11,281	0.2000
1939	183	84,901	1.50	27,040	0.4774

Source: Annual Reports, Secretary, United States Savings and Loan League.

were reports of state supervisory departments, and in many cases these were inadequate. One handicap in studying depression losses based upon published supervisory reports is the lack of consistency in publishing the record of associations placed in receivership or liquidation. Many associations underwent substantial reorganization, some disappeared completely, and the most sizable losses were suffered by institutions which were dissolved and of which no published record exists.

In an effort to obtain a fair and complete picture of the extent of depression losses in the savings and loan business, a detailed tracing was undertaken of a number of institutions which were in business at the beginning of the depression. The Research Department of the United States Savings and Loan League conducted a study of the depression experience of associations in Milwaukee, Wisconsin; Kansas City, Missouri; and in California, Indiana, Michigan, and West Virginia. Altogether, 539 institutions were studied on a year-by-year basis covering the 1930's.

Table 9-2 summarizes the results of the loss analysis of 539 associations in these six areas. Almost 16 percent of the associations showed losses of 20 percent or more of their 1930 mortgage balances, while 25 percent showed losses of 15 percent or more, and altogether, 35 percent revealed

TABLE 9-2
Depression Loss Experience
Savings and Loan Associations in
Milwaukee, Wis.; Kansas City, Mo.; and in
California, Indiana, Michigan, and West Virginia
(Total Loss as Percentage of 1930 Mortgage Loan Balance)

Percentage of Loss to 1930 Mortgage Loan Balance	Savings Associations		Asset Distribution	
	Number	Percentage of Total	1930 Assets (Thousands)	Percentage of Total
Less than 5%	271	50.3%	$ 411,673	36.9%
5% and less than 10%	77	14.3	165,116	14.8
10% and less than 15%	53	9.8	154,580	13.9
15% and less than 20%	53	9.8	111,442	10.0
20% and over	85	15.8	271,585	24.4
Total	539	100.0%	$1,114,396	100.0%

The institutions covered in the above tabulation comprise the major portion of all savings and and loan associations in the areas indicated. The sources used were the published reports of supervisory authorities as well as the records in the files of those officials; numerous personal interviews were also made. The analysis involved a year-by-year loss study covering the decade of the 1930's for each institution. The Research Department of the United States Savings and Loan League has a copy of the case study of each association included in the study except for those in California. The California research was done by the Savings and Loan Commissioner of California.

losses of 10 percent or more. The 539 associations reported assets at the outset of the depression amounting to $1.1 billion. Over 24 percent of the assets were those of institutions showing losses of 20 percent or over and 34 percent were those of associations with losses of 15 percent or over. Altogether, almost half (48 percent) of the aggregate assets were represented by institutions suffering losses of 10 percent or over.

Losses to Savers

Although the statistics represent an accurate record of the major losses suffered by associations in these five areas, there were others which cannot be measured—those losses experienced by the savers and borrowers, the most common type being that suffered by the saver who desired cash immediately and sold his passbook in the open market. Although many associations were disbursing limited amounts to their savers, some savers needed additional cash and took what they could get at the time by selling their passbooks. In some cities a well-organized market for the shares of building and loan associations developed, and quote sheets similar to those appearing for common stocks on the financial pages of today's newspapers were published by brokerage firms. Table 9-3 is a copy of an offering sheet published by W. L. Rittel and Company of Milwaukee on May 1, 1936. It shows rather clearly that shares usually were sold at discounts of 20 percent to 30 percent, and is submitted as evidence that some savers took substantial losses on their accounts.

Another loss to savers during the depression years resulted from the

TABLE 9-3
Building and Loan Stocks—May 1, 1936
Milwaukee, Wisconsin

	Approx. Market		Approx. Market
Acme	65-67	Liberty	67-70
Advance	69-71	Lincoln	57-60
Aetna	75-77	Lisbon Avenue	40-42
Alliance	38-39	Marquette	85-88
Arrow	35-38	Metropolitan	78-80
Assurance	26-28	Milwaukee Mid-City	69-71
Atlas	72-75	Mitchell Street	72-74
Badger	78-81	Modern Mutual	74-76
Bahn Frel	65-68	Mutual	80-82
Bay View	69-72	National	77-78
Ben Franklin	81-83	North Avenue	82-84
Biltmore	69-70	North Shore	84-85
Bluemound	65-68	Northern	85-87
Capitol	47-50	Northwestern	88-90
Center Street	42-44	Peoples	71-73
Central	18-20	Pioneer	67-69
Citizens' Mutual	87-90	Progressive	65-68
City Savings	30-33	Prosperity	68-71
Civic Mutual	61-63	Pulaski	74-78
Columbia	60-62	Pyramid	69-71
Community	73-75	Reliance	79-81
Concordia	71-74	Republic	69-71
County	53-55	Residence Park	67-70
Cream City	47-50	Riverside	69-71
Cudahy Savings	53-55	St. Francis	83-86
East Side	75-77	Second Bohemian	74-77
Economy	68-70	Security	79-82
Equitable	74-75	Sentry	70-71
Excelsior	81-83	Sherman Park	80-82
Fidelity	80-81	Slovak	52-54
First Bohemian	74-76	Sobieski	48-51
First Slovak	73-76	South Side Mutual	77-79
Forward	65-68	Standard	78-80
Great Lakes	38-40	State	57-60
Green Bay Avenue	83-85	Sterling	72-75
Greenfield Avenue	61-63	Suburban	72-74
Guardian	62-64	Tippecanoe	15-18
Guaranty	57-60	United	77-78
Highland Park	82-85	Upper Third	66-69
Holton Street	66-69	Washington	64-66
Home Mutual	70-72	Wauwatosa	78-80
Hopkins Street	85-88	Waukesha Savings	74-76
Integrity	74-76	Waukesha Ind.	74-76
Jackson	55-58	Welfare	66-67
Keystone Mutual	67-69	West Allis	80-82
Kinnickinnic	72-74	West Side	65-68
Lakeside	65-67	White Eagle	74-76
Layton Park	78-80	Wisconsin Savings	79-80

Source: Quotation Sheet of W. L. Rittel & Co., Milwaukee, Wisconsin.

fact that, almost without exception, associations reduced their dividend rates considerably. Whereas in the late 1920's the typical dividend rate was 5 percent to 6 percent, in the early 1930's the rates were 2 percent to 3 percent, and many associations paid no dividends whatever.

Losses were particularly severe in the case of mortgage-pledged shares, that is, share accounts which were being accumulated by the saver as a sinking fund in order to pay off his loan. The interest rate of the loan had been set in anticipation of a 5 percent to 6 percent dividend rate, but when the dividend rate was substantially reduced, the effective cost to the borrower for his loan was increased proportionately, possibly causing further difficulty.

Remedies Adopted

Federal Home Loan Bank System

An important development designed to remedy weaknesses in the savings and loan business was the establishment of the Federal Home Loan Bank System. Although a central reserve system for savings institutions engaged in home mortgage finance was considered earlier, it was not until the onset of the depression that the System was instituted. In December 1931, a Conference on Home Building and Home Ownership was called by President Herbert Hoover. Following the recommendation of the President, the Conference approved the organization of the Federal Home Loan Bank System. A bill providing for the creation of a central reserve credit system for savings institutions engaged in home mortgage finance was promptly introduced and passed by Congress in 1932.

The contributions which the Federal Home Loan Bank System made to the promotion of confidence and stability in the savings and home financing area are described in the following passage:

> The economic environment of the early and middle 1930's provided an immediate opportunity to the Federal Home Loan Bank System to demonstrate its usefulness. The heavy withdrawals of savings in that period had all but dried up the supply of home mortgage funds. By advancing funds to its member savings and home financing institutions, this reserve credit system did more than make new funds available for home loans. It made funds available to meet withdrawals of savings promptly, thereby helping to restore confidence in the member savings institutions, and attracting a new flow of savings.[1]

Home Owners Loan Corporation

In 1933, Congress authorized the creation of the Home Owners Loan

---

[1] Carl F. Distelhorst, "Savings and Loan Associations and Mutual Savings Banks," in *American Financial Institutions,* Herbert V. Prochnow, ed. (New York, 1951), p. 139.

Corporation under the direction of the Home Loan Bank Board. Through this program, about one-sixth of the urban home mortgage debt was transferred from private lending agencies, including savings and loan associations, to the HOLC during the period from June 1933 to June 1936. The objective was to refinance these loans on easier terms so that families threatened with losing their homes could retain possession by arranging for a smaller payment on their passbooks.

The aggregate losses of the HOLC were $336,562,852 on a total of 198,215 defaulted loans which the Corporation foreclosed. Since the Corporation made 1,017,821 loans, for a total amount of $3,093,451,321,[2] HOLC losses were approximately 11 percent of the total amount of loans made.

In considering the depression losses on the home mortgage business as measured by the experience of the Home Owners Loan Corporation, it is necessary to add to the 11 percent figure mentioned above, the "write-down" on loans taken over by the Corporation. As quoted from page 70 of the Sixth Annual Report of the Federal Home Loan Bank Board:

> In many instances, the mortgage debts originally owned by HOLC borrowers were scaled down in the process of refinancing. In all, it is estimated that this reduction was in the neighborhood of $200 million or about 7 percent of the original debt.

Thus, the record of the Home Owners Loan Corporation indicates that the total losses in the mortgage business were approximately 18 percent.

An additional loss which associations suffered on transferring mortgages to the HOLC resulted when associations sold the bonds of the Corporation. Because these bonds were not guaranteed by the U.S. Treasury as to principal and interest, they had a market value less than par. This difference must be considered as a loss.

Other Measures

In 1934, Congress provided for the creation of the Federal Savings and Loan Insurance Corporation. This helped to restore confidence in the savings and loan business in much the same manner in which confidence had been restored in the commercial banking system a year earlier through the creation of the Federal Deposit Insurance Corporation.

That same year, Congress also authorized the use of mortgage insurance through the Federal Housing Administration. FHA-insured loans, Congress hoped, would bring funds back into the residential real estate market and thereby stimulate the home construction industry. By revising the mortgage lending practices of the 1920's so that longer maturities, lower down payments, and smaller monthly payments on loans might

---

[2] Final Report to the Congress of the United States relating to the Home Owners Loan Corporation, March 1, 1952, p. 4.

become more readily available to home purchasers and builders, congressional leaders hoped to push the economy back on the growth track.

While these developments were occurring in home financing techniques, equally important changes were taking place within the savings and loan business itself. In 1933, Congress provided for the Federal Savings and Loan System as Section 5 of the Home Owners Loan Act. Following this lead, many states modified, revised, and improved their state savings and loan codes in order to provide greater flexibility and uniformity of operation. For example, by the late 1930's most associations had shifted their method of loan repayment to the direct reduction plan. Prior to that time, although loans were amortized, loan payments often were accumulated in savings accounts and periodically credited to the loan balances.

Chapter 10

ROLE IN THE ECONOMIC
AND FINANCIAL SYSTEM

One of the principal advantages of a free economic system is that it has flexibility and can adapt to current needs. It brings out the most creative aspects of the individual and maximizes his productivity and his ability to contribute to society. Fortunately, the efforts of individuals to maximize their money income have the general effect of maximizing the real economic product and the national welfare. As long as the individual rather than the state remains the focal point in our system, most of the important economic decisions will be made individually. In the world of finance, as elsewhere, consumers and businessmen must be free to choose the institutions which best serve their needs and be free to design new techniques and raise to prominence new institutions if and when the existing structure no longer suffices.

Finance may be considered a facilitating function in our economic system. Its aim is to enhance the efficient creation of form, time, place, and possession utilities. The world of finance is composed of a dynamic and constantly evolving framework of institutions, techniques, and instruments. As businessmen and consumers develop new needs or seek goods and services in new forms, the way must be kept open for innovation and experimentation in finance as well as elsewhere. The various devices for exchanging goods and services for money, together with the various steps that channel savings into investments, may be considered the vehicle on which our financial and economic system flows. At times, the role of government may loom relatively large in the affairs of the financial community (e.g., during war or depression). At other times, government's role may be reduced in accordance with the changed conditions in the economic setting.

Savings and loan associations function in harmony with the precepts of a free economic system. They have gained substantial acceptance by consumers and businessmen because they have been able to satisfy efficiently and effectively an urgent consumer need. At the end of

148

World War II, only the question of economic stability—eliminating serious depression from our system—held a higher priority among domestic problems than that of housing the American people. Given this need and the depression-related reluctance of other institutional lenders to allot increasing portions of their funds to mortgages on individual residential properties, savings associations were bound to prosper, for they were committed exclusively to this area. Under free market conditions, associations were able to attract a sufficient volume of savings funds into the home financing field so that government participation in housing was limited basically to insurance and guarantee techniques.

A growing economy needs a large volume of savings in order to achieve growth without inflation. Savings and loan associations—established in adequate numbers, located conveniently, and offering savers thrift plans and programs with broad appeal—are able to aid in achieving this goal. Associations seek to stimulate thrift in fair weather and foul, when investment returns are high and when they are low. By offering an attractive return to savers and raising the desirability of saving in the estimation of the American people, associations have aided the accumulation of long-term capital. The strong desire of association managers to curry favor among savers has been an important factor in their success as solicitors of savings funds. At commercial banks the time-deposit service until recently was relegated to a sideline position in the view of bank management, and success in inducing savings has not been nearly as pronounced as at the savings associations. Because they may be a sideline, bank time deposits are given support when money becomes tight and interest rates are rising or high, but are not promoted when interest rates are falling and money becomes easy. This difference in attitudes between the specialized savings institution and the departmentalized financial institutions is significant.

In order to continue to stimulate savings in the future, savings and loan associations are presently studying their savings product intensively with a view to tailoring their savings account more closely to individual thrift preferences.

In the past, individuals in the higher income brackets traditionally did most of the saving and provided most of the venture capital. Today, as savings become democratized and institutionalized, those in the middle and lower income brackets are the originators of a sizable pool of savings. Because these people tend to channel their funds through institutions rather than into venture capital, some question arises as to whether the institutional concentration of capital funds might not seriously affect the existing private enterprise system and significantly reshape our social order. Institutions, it is maintained, are by nature conservative and prone to avoid marginal risks. To the extent that these shifts represent the result of free choices on the part of consumers and as long as the door is kept open to innovation in the world of finance, such an allocation of funds is appropriate to our American system of creative capitalism.

Professor Jules Bogen of New York University, as well as other students of the subject, maintains that he can see no evidence that the American people have shown any lessening of attachment to institutional savings as the favored medium of investment.[1] The liquidity, safety, and flexibility of the savings account is preferred by most people. The one exception that might be cited is when substantially higher yields are offered on short- and intermediate-term United States government obligations, as in the case of the "Magic Fives" in 1959. During the decade of the 1960's, Professor Bogen maintains, institutions will continue to be the chief channel through which personal savings flow into the various sectors of investment. If this is so, then the credit needs of the American economy in the home financing area can be expected to be met in large and growing measure by savings and loan associations, the "specialty shop" assigned to that area by Congress and the state legislatures.

Role in the Investment Market

The specialized role played by savings and loan associations in the network of financial institutions restricts their activity to a single corner of the capital market. Such a role is in keeping with the local character of the home mortgage business and the need to have pools of funds available for home financing in large and small urban centers of the nation. The financing of existing properties is just as vital to a sound real estate market as is the financing of new units. Because the mortgage process is complex and the risks on any one property may be considerable, individuals find the extension of such funds hazardous. However, by placing dollars with a savings and loan association, an individual may hire experienced and supervised professional mortgage lenders to place funds in a home mortgage, and benefit from a wider degree of diversification than might otherwise be possible. In short, associations provide a means for transferring and minimizing risks. Experience is substituted for inexperience, and diversification is substituted for concentration. The individual saver or investor is also relieved of the problems of personal supervision of his investment.

There is some criticism of savings and loan associations because of the inflexibility of their investment powers; a rigid policy of investment in home mortgages, it is maintained, impedes the free flow of funds in our economy. Such a thesis may overlook the fact that a financial system can have too much flexibility. Funds could completely pass over certain types of investment and certain localities as their owners or managers seek

---

[1] *1960 Proceedings Conference on Savings and Residential Financing* (Chicago: United States Savings & Loan League), pp. 100-119.

to maximize earnings and opportunities for profit. There is a very real danger that the shift of funds with full freedom among alternate investment opportunities may result in the abandonment of the residential mortgage market in many localities.

In order to keep the local real estate markets of the country in a relatively liquid condition, funds must be available at a reasonable cost to support the sale of existing real estate; to permit additions or alterations to property; and for small loans, refinancing, and other purposes. The financial system should be designed to care for these needs and to protect the consumer and the nation against the too free flow of funds into or out of the local housing markets. Although the freeing of the flow of mortgage funds is a desirable goal, it should not go too far.

The economic stability of communities and their real estate base are protected by the existence of savings associations prepared to lend regularly in the local market. The specialized character of residential home mortgage financing dictates a specialized and separate institutional facility to care for this need. Evidence from other parts of the world seems to indicate that the urban mortgage loan is a type of finance which can be handled most efficiently by specialized institutions. The Crédit Foncier of France and the Hypotheken Banks of Germany are Western European examples.

The history of the development of financial institutions in this country indicates that as the type of loan becomes more complex and volume increases, specialized lending institutions grow in number. Differences in lending and appraisal procedures and techniques were among the more important elements leading to the establishment of specialized financial institutions in the fields of farm credit, consumer credit, and home financing credit. Savings associations, functioning as experts in lending procedures and techniques of home financing, are in closer contact with local real estate markets and may well be better able to pass on the credit risks and other requirements of the specialized loan.

Another advantage the "specialty shop" may have over the institution which renders numerous services is an independence and clarity of judgment regarding lending in a particular area. What might be termed tie-in sales seem to have considerable attraction at multi-service financial institutions. For example, in the 1920's, commercial banks having security affiliates tended to give preferred status in their lending operations to securities underwritten and sold by their affiliates. In addition, the trust departments of commercial banks preferred to hold securities underwritten and sold by the corporate affiliate. In each of these cases, the independent appraisal of market risks was blurred.

The use of financial intermediaries to carry long-term debt aids economic stability by tying any sharp jumps in such debt to savings. Thus, cyclical swings in business are less aggravated than if the mortgage debt became part of the portfolio of commercial banks and thus were monetized. This is true even if savings are increased by transfers of idle demand deposits to savings and loan associations. Velocity will increase, it is true, and this is equivalent to an increase in the volume of money. But, the extent to which velocity can increase is limited, assuming a controlled money supply. Sooner or later individuals find they have a liquidity need, and transfers of additional amounts of demand deposits to savings cease.

The Flow of Funds

The savings and loan business in its modern-day evolution has within its powers a number of devices designed to facilitate the free flow of funds. Other factors impede the flow of funds. For summary purposes, both sets of factors are listed below.

Factors Facilitating the Flow of Funds	Factors Impeding the Flow of Funds
FHLB advances	Local character of associations
Participation loan program	Size of associations
Insurance of accounts	Limit on lending radius
Purchase and sale of mortgages	Laws and traditions

Note that the factors designed to facilitate the free flow of funds are all aimed at smoothing that flow geographically, that is, from one region of the country or one locale to another. None is designed, as in the case of other lending institutions, to shift funds from the housing market to other investment outlets.

Tax Incentives as a Stimulus to Economic Growth and Stability

One technique for stimulating savings would be an income tax concession on earnings accruing from institutional savings. Such a technique has been used with considerable success in other parts of the world. Germany, for example, following World War II, helped stimulate investment and capital goods by granting tax concessions to savers. In Canada, wage earners are allowed to put aside for retirement 10 percent of their annual earned income to a maximum of $2,500; no taxes are levied on this sum, and it may be invested in government bonds, stocks, savings accounts, etc., as the wage earner sees fit.

The basic philosophy behind such plans to encourage thrift is not without precedent in the United States. The typical retirement plan in an American industrial or commercial firm includes a tax benefit on that portion of the fund which is contributed by the firm. Another manifestation of this concept in American society is the ability of individuals saving through life insurance to have these funds passed on to their heirs after death without any taxation. The government thus encourages and aids individuals to save and provide for their families and dependents.

TABLE 10-1

Savings Incentive Techniques Employed during the 1950's
Selected Countries

Country	Tax Exemption or Other Benefit on: Income Saved	Earnings on Savings	Savings for Home Purchases	Retirement Funds	Long-Term Savings	Savings by Young Persons	Indexation: Savings Funds Linked to Price Level	Lottery Savings or Bonds	Special Fiscal Privileges for Savings Institutions
Austria	X	X	X				X	X	X
Belgium		X		X					
Canada	X	X		X					X
Denmark				X		X	X		
Finland	X	X			X		X		
France	X	X	X	X	X		X	X	
Germany	X	X	X		X		X	X	
Greece	X	X			X		X		X
Israel	X	X	X		X		X	X	
Italy	X	X	X		X				
Japan		X						X	X
Netherlands				X	X	X		X	X
Norway		X			X	X		X	X
Sweden	X	X			X	X		X	
Switzerland		X						X	
Turkey	X	X		X					
United Kingdom		X			X			X	

The indications in this table refer to plans effected during the 1950's. Some savings incentive schemes have been repealed, others revised, and still others further supplemented.

Sources: "Personal Saving and Its Promotion," Banks for International Settlements, Basle, Switzerland, April 1958; Bank of Japan, "Role of Savings in Japan's Postwar Growth," Economic Bulletin for Asia and the Far East, September 1960; Various reports from Savings and Central Banks of Europe and the Near East.

If public policy requires higher levels of saving and investment on the part of the American people in order to promote economic growth, then the possibilities of using tax incentives to stimulate the accumulation of capital funds at savings institutions should not be overlooked. Table 10-1 summarizes the various methods free world nations have employed to encourage thrift.

Population, Income, and Savings

In order to test statistically the relationship between trends at savings associations and the broad movement of economic activity in this country, a series of correlations was undertaken. The correlation between changes in population nationally and changes in savings at savings and loan associations was positive. As population gains increased, so did gains in savings at associations. The correlation coefficient was 0.82.

There was also positive correlation between the level of total disposable personal income and total savings at savings and loan associations during the past thirty years. When year-to-year changes in disposable personal income are compared to year-to-year changes in savings at associations, however, little correlation appears. Years of strong economic growth and rising income apparently are also years of rising consumer confidence and lower levels of liquid savings. For example, during prosperous periods such as 1948, 1950-51, 1955, and 1956-57, strong gains took place in disposable personal income, but savings at associations rose moderately or not at all. During years when the income of Americans rose relatively little (1949, 1954, and 1959), savings at associations increased. Apparently, once again, consumer attitudes were at work. The coefficient of correlation between changes in disposable personal income and changes in savings at associations was a low 0.06.

Housing, Households, and Mortgage Lending

The willingness of Americans to contract mortgage debt has permitted savings and loan associations to grow. In general, associations grew most rapidly in areas where population gains, especially immigration of new families, was strongest. The coefficient of correlation between private non-farm residential construction and mortgage lending at associations was 0.98.

Another broad area where correlation techniques were applied was the relationship between mortgage lending activity at savings associations and the level of household formations. A test of annual household formations and mortgage lending at associations produced no correlation. The coefficient was 0.16. However, a positive correlation did appear when a ten-year lag was introduced into the data. Since the typical household formation occurs at the age of marriage, generally twenty years old, the addition of ten years places the critical age for home buying and the making of a mortgage contract at approximately thirty years. When the correlation is run on this basis, the relationship improves noticeably, and a coefficient of correlation of 0.86 results. Household formations, however, are not the only factor bearing on the lending activity at savings associations. The availability and cost of mortgage funds, the existence or nonexistence of a backlog of housing demand, shifts in migratory movements of families, and many other factors have a bearing on the situation.

A Final Observation

The function of finance in the American economic system is to facilitate the transfer of goods and services. Its basic purpose is to enhance the dynamism of a creative capitalism, not to control it. Financial institutions and the process through which goods and services are transferred in a money economy should not be the tail that wags the dog. The financial system should have built into it the degree of control necessary to provide economic growth without inflation, but it should never be so restrictive as to preclude innovations and inventions in the world of finance. Although formalized research in finance is not typically undertaken in the same way that it is in science or commercial enterprises, certainly the philosophy of innovation implicit in the research expenditures of American industry ought to serve as well in the field of finance.

Hence, although control has an important place in the American financial system, there must be sufficient flexibility or adaptability in the system so that if and when the controllers err, they will not jeopardize the capacity for innovation in financial arrangements. The possibility of birth and death among financial institutions must continue to exist. It may be tempered only to the degree necessary to safeguard the assets of the community. Under such a philosophy, and within the network of financial institutions, savings and loan associations operate as efficient allocators of funds for home finance.

Appendix A

STATE LIMITATIONS ON
CONVENTIONAL MORTGAGE LOANS

A review of statutory provisions relating to state savings associations in the various states covering (1) maximum ratio of loan to value, (2) maximum maturity of the conventional mortgage loan, and (3) maximum amount of loan.

Prepared by
the Legal Department
of the
UNITED STATES SAVINGS AND LOAN LEAGUE
Chicago 1, Illinois

September 1, 1961

State Limitations on Conventional Mortgage Loans

State	% of Loan to Value	Maximum Maturity	Maximum Amount of Loan	Statute Reference
Alabama		20 yrs.	$20,000 except when made under 30% of capital lending power	S & L Law, Title 5, Secs. 211, 230
Alaska			$45,000	Sec. 23, Alaska Sav. Assn. Act
Arizona	Assn. Insured - 75% Assn. Uninsured - 60%	-	-	Arizona Code Ann., Sec. 51-607
Arkansas			Loan Limited To: / If Assets Do Not Exceed: $5,000 / $50,000 10,000 / 200,000 15,000 / 500,000 Limit of $25,000 to one borrower except that Assns. with assets in excess of $5,000,000 may loan not to exceed 1% of assets to one borrower.	Arkansas Stats. Ann., Sec. 67-831
California	Appraised Value Under $15,000 - 80% Appraisal in Excess of $15,000 - 70%	25 yrs.	$20,000 if loan exceeds 1% of book value of assets.	Financial Code, Secs. 7150-7154, as amended by S.B. 694, Laws 1955; Sec. 7162
Colorado	-	20 yrs.	Loans in excess of $50,000 to maximum aggregate of 20% of gross assets.	Colorado Rev. Stats., Sec. 122-2-19
Connecticut	80% 90%	25 yrs. 30 yrs.	$20,000	Banking Law, Ch. 282, Sec. 5894(h)
Delaware	-	30 yrs.	-	Delaware Code Ann., Ch. 19, Sec. 1905, as amended by S.B. 356, Laws 1955

State	%	Term	Loan Limit	Statute
District of Columbia	–	–	–	D.C. Code, Title 26, Secs. 26-406, 26-407
Florida	Members – Nonmembers - 70%	–	$25,000 on one property except not exceeding 20%-of-assets may be loaned without regard to $25,000 limitation.	Florida Law, Title XXXVII, Ch. 665, Sec. 665.21
Georgia	80%	25 yrs.	–	B & L Act, Rule 10, pursuant to Sec. 8.
Hawaii	80% / 90% (similar to Federal Lending Powers)	–	$50,000	Sec. 180-60, Rev. Laws
Idaho	–	–	–	Idaho Code, Sec. 30-1304
Illinois	–	–	–	S & L Act, Secs. 5-1, 5-4
Indiana	80% / 90% (similar to Federal Lending Powers)	Weekly or Monthly Installments - 25 yrs.	2% of total assets to one borrower except as follows: Loan Not to Exceed: Assets: $250,000 or less — $5,000; $250,000 to $375,000 — $7,500; $375,000 or more — $10,000 or 2% of total assets, whichever is greater	B & L Law, Secs. 273, 275, and 276, Part 5, Art. 1
Iowa	80% / 90%	25 yrs	$35,000 (Loans in excess of $35,000 subject to 30% of assets limit)	Iowa Code 1950, Sec. 534.32, as amended by H.B. 228, Laws '55
Kansas	–	30 yrs.	$35,000 except under 30% of capital lending power.	Kansas Stats. 17-5101 i, 17-5501, as amended by H.B. 199, Laws 1955

State Limitations on Conventional Mortgage Loans (Continued)

State	% of Loan to Value	Maximum Maturity	Maximum Amount of Loan	Statute Reference
Kentucky	-	-	Bylaws may restrict maximum amount.	Kentucky Law, Ch. 289, Secs. 289.180, 289.190
Louisiana	Lending plans must be approved by Commissioner, including maximum percent and amortization period.		$50,000 except on authorization and affirmative vote of 2/3 of all board members. Assn. is limited also to 3% of capital or $10,000 whichever is greater.	Homestead & B & L Laws, Secs. 6:756, 6:887
Maine	80% (1- to 4-family homes) 70% (other improved property)	25 yrs. 20 yrs.	One property: $25,000 or 10% of surplus funds. One borrower: $35,000 or 20% of surplus funds.	Banking Laws, Ch. 59, Sec. 167
Maryland	-	-	-	Maryland Law, Art 23, Sec. 148
Massachusetts	80% (75% for loans over $20,000 and not exceeding $25,000) 90% (similar to Federal Lending Powers)	20 yrs.	$25,000 (Aggregate of loans whose unpaid balance is more than $20,000 shall not exceed 20% of assets of corporation).	General Laws, Ch. 170, Sec. 24, as amended by H.B. 2596, Ch. 96, Laws 1958
Michigan	3/4 (75%)	-	Limited as to directors, officers, and employees: $50,000 or 2% of assets whichever is less.	Michigan Stats. Ann., Sec. 23.548
Minnesota	% shall be fixed in the bylaws.	25 yrs.	May be fixed in bylaws.	S B & L Act, Secs. 51.01, 51.34, 51.43
Mississippi	-	-	-	Miss. Law, Sec. 5296
Missouri	-	-	$35,000	S & L Law, Sec. 369.360, amended 1955

State	Loan %	Term	Loan Limited to	Statute
Montana	75%	-	-	Montana Stats. Title 7, Sec. 7-113(13)
Nebraska	3/4 (75%) / 90%	-	Assets: / Loan Limited to: To $200,000 — $10,000 $200,000 to $500,000 — $20,000 $500,000 to $1 Million — $30,000 $1 Million to $3 Million — $40,000 $3 Million to $5 Million — $50,000 $5 Million — $75,000	Banking Laws, Ch. 8, Art. 3, Secs. 8-303, 8-319
Nevada	80%	25 yrs.	$35,000 (Over $35,000 loans included in a 30%-of-assets limitation.	Nevada Compiled Laws, Secs. 954, 970; S.B. 112, Ch. 396, Sec. 13, Laws 1957
New Hampshire	Amount of Loan / Percent Appraisal Value Under $10,000 — — $10,000-20,000 — 80% Excess of $20,000 — 70%	20 yrs.	$10,000 except: if mortgage loan aggregate exceeds $500,000, amount of a loan may be 2½% of assets or $15,000 whichever is greater; in no event shall loan exceed $20,000 or ½ of 1%, whichever is greater.	New Hampshire B & L Laws, Secs. 10, 13
New Jersey	80%	25 yrs.	$25,000 or 2½% of assets, whichever is greater.	S & L Act, Art. X, Sec. 78, as amended by Assembly Bill 424, Laws 1955, and Sec. 82
New Mexico	90% (similar to Federal Lending Powers)	-	-	B & L Laws, Secs. 5 & 6

State Limitations on Conventional Mortgage Loans (Continued)

State	% of Loan to Value	Maximum Maturity	Maximum Amount of Loan	Statute Reference
New York	90% (On Owner-Occupied, 1- to 2-family Dwellings less than 10 Years Old) 80%	25 yrs. 75% of Life of Building or 30 Years, whichever is less.	$25,000	Banking Law, Secs. 379 and 380 as amended by Sen. Int. 1246, Laws 1955; Assembly Int. 4378, Laws 1958, adding subdiv. 1-a to Sec. 380
North Carolina	-	25 yrs.	-	N.C. Law, CH. 54, Sec. 54-20
North Dakota	75% 90%	-	Assets: / Loan Not To Exceed — To $50,000: $5,000; $50,000 to $100,000: $7,500; $100,000 to $200,000: $10,000; $200,000 to $500,000: $15,000; Over $500,000: 3% of Assets. Loan exceeding $20,000 must be approved by 2/3 of Board of Directors.	North Dakota Law, Title 7, Sec. 7.0413
Ohio	75% (May be Increased to 80% by Stockholders.) 90% (similar to Federal Lending Powers)	25 yrs.	$35,000	B & L Law, Sec. 9657, as amended by H.B. 203, Laws 1955
Oklahoma	Manner and Terms upon which Loans Shall Be Made and Repaid Shall Be Determined by the Bylaws.			Oklahoma Stats. Title 18, Secs. 215, 233
Oregon	80% (90% if Excess Reserve Fund set up.)	25 yrs.	5% of total assets on one property. (Assns. with assets up to $100,000 may lend up to $5,000 on one property.)	Oregon Laws, Ch. 722, Secs. 722.410, 722.455-450
Pennsylvania	80%	-	1- to 4-family property: $25,000; 5- to 6-family property: $40,000	B & L Code, Art. IX, Sec. 903

State	%	Term	Loan/Asset Limit	Citation
Rhode Island	-	25 yrs.	-	B & L Law, Ch. 158, Sec. 14
South Carolina	80	-	-	Banking Laws, Title 8, Ch. 6, Dec. 8-603
South Dakota	80% (50% of loans outside 100 mile radius.)	-	Loans exceeding $20,000 be approved by 2/3 of the Board of Directors.	Banking Law, Title 7, Sec. 7-0403, as amended by S.B. 103, Laws 1955
Tennessee	2/3 (66 2/3 %)	20 yrs.	-	B & L Laws, Secs. 3901, 3905.1
Texas	80% (More than 4-Family: 65%)	25 yrs.	Assets: To $50,000 / $50,000-$200,000 / $200,000-$500,000 / Over $500,000 — Loan: $5,000 / 10,000 / 20,000 / 50,000 / Or, 2% of assets, whichever is greater.	Vernon's Code Ann., Secs. 881a-37, 881a-25
Utah	80%	-	$35,000	Utah Code, Ch. 5, Secs. 7-7-1, 7-7-5, as amended by S.B. 64, Laws 1955
Vermont	-	20 yrs.	$25,000	Vermont Stats. Ch. 384, Secs. 8935-8940, as amended by S.B. 128, Laws 1957
Virginia	90%	25 yrs.	$35,000	Code of Virginia, 1950 Ch. 3, Art. 5, Sec. 6-168
Washington	Age of Dwelling — % / New to 30 mos. 80% / To 15 yrs. 66 2/3% / Others 50-60%	25 yrs.	-	Revised Code of Washington, Sec. 33.24-100

(Notwithstanding this section, an association may make any loan permitted to a Federal savings and loan association doing business in this state.)

State Limitations on Conventional Mortgage Loans (Continued)

State	% of Loan to Value	Maximum Maturity	Maximum Amount of Loan	Statute Reference
West Virginia	75%	20 yrs.	-	West Virginia Code of 1955, Sec. 3164 (12) (14)
Wisconsin	Loans in excess of $50,000 not to exceed 65%	30 yrs.	Assets: — Loan Limit to One Borrower Less than $50,000 — $ 5,000 $50,001 to $100,000 — $ 7,500 $100,001 to $200,000 — $10,000 $200,001 to $500,000 — $20,000 $500,001 to $1,000,000 — $25,000 In Excess of $1,000,000 — 5% of Assets	Wisconsin Stats., Ch. 215, Sec. 215.22, as amended by S.B. 65, Laws 1955
Wyoming	65%	-	-	Wyoming Stats., Ch. 36, Sec. 36-110

Appendix B

ADJUSTMENT FOR SEASONAL
VARIATION—METHODOLOGY

Seasonally Adjusted Data on Savings and Lending
at Savings and Loan Associations, 1946 to 1960

In the analysis of time series, it may be desirable to use some kind of curve to describe the trend of the series. Use of such a curve will facilitate the measurement of seasonal, cyclical, and any other variations from the trend. The moving average is a simple method—and one of the most flexible mathematical methods—of smoothing the seasonal variations in a time series. In fitting a trend line to monthly data on gross savings, withdrawals, net savings, and mortgage lending, a twelve-month moving average was selected in order to eliminate any direct or inverse bias in the analysis of monthly data unadjusted for seasonal variation. The steps taken in the computation of a twelve-month moving average are:

1) Obtain twelve-month moving totals.
2) Obtain two-month totals of the twelve-month totals, (in order to center the data on specific months).
3) Divide the figures obtained in Step 2 by twenty-four, which results in centered twelve-month moving averages.
4) Divide the original data by the twelve-month moving averages to obtain a series of ratios of the original data to the moving averages.

Seasonal and irregular influences are smoothed out in the twelve-month moving average obtained in Step 3, leaving the effects of secular and cyclical changes. By dividing the original data by the twelve-month moving average, these secular and cyclical influences are removed, leaving seasonal and irregular influences in the ratio-to-moving-average figures obtained.

The next problem is the removal of the irregular influences. A positional mean, combining some of the advantages of both a median and an

165

arithmetic average, is computed. The first step in obtaining a positional mean is to array the ratio-to-moving-average figures by months. Since it is reasonable to assume that irregular influences and any cyclical influences remaining in the ratios would cause those ratios to fall at the extremes of the array, the influence of such factors on the seasonal index is reduced by eliminating the items at both extremes in the array. In this case the four largest and four smallest items in each monthly column are eliminated and an average of the four middle items is obtained. The last step (unnecessary in this instance) is to adjust the positional means to total 1,200.

The series of twelve index numbers which has now been obtained can be used to adjust raw data for seasonal variation. The plotting of these indices will show typical seasonal variation in gross savings at savings and loan associations.

The seasonally adjusted totals on a monthly basis from 1946 to 1960 for gross savings, withdrawals, net savings, and mortgage lending at savings and loan associations follow.

TABLE B-1
Gross Savings at Savings and Loan Associations
1947-1960

(Seasonally adjusted, millions of dollars)

Month	1947	1948	1949	1950	1951	1952	1953	1954	1955	1956	1957	1958	1959	1960
January	$273	$304	$354	$404	$489	$600	$734	$ 853	$1044	$1245	$1360	$1475	$1732	$1969
February	273	310	356	409	503	609	748	865	1064	1267	1366	1483	1733	1978
March	275	313	358	414	511	617	756	876	1082	1274	1373	1496	1792	1997
April	277	315	361	422	517	627	765	885	1100	1281	1383	1515	1809	2015
May	279	317	364	432	522	634	773	896	1117	1289	1389	1531	1824	2031
June	281	321	367	439	530	645	781	913	1132	1298	1397	1550	1841	2048
July	286	328	372	448	542	663	792	935	1156	1314	1410	1573	1875	2065
August	290	335	376	456	555	675	803	955	1178	1328	1418	1589	1907	2079
September	292	340	381	459	565	685	814	970	1187	1333	1427	1605	1923	2098
October	294	344	386	464	573	697	824	985	1197	1340	1439	1629	1936	2119
November	295	348	391	470	580	706	832	1001	1209	1346	1450	1652	1946	2141
December	298	352	398	477	589	718	842	1021	1222	1352	1463	1677	1961	2170

Source: Based on data published by Federal Home Loan Bank Board.

167

TABLE B-2
Withdrawals from Savings and Loan Associations
1947–1960

(Seasonally adjusted, millions of dollars)

Month	1947	1948	1949	1950	1951	1952	1953	1954	1955	1956	1957	1958	1959	1960
January	$176	$211	$239	$280	$359	$373	$445	$520	$651	$820	$ 952	$1019	$1183	$1398
February	178	218	240	292	359	379	457	529	674	841	968	1017	1216	1405
March	179	221	242	300	358	383	464	536	690	848	975	1021	1233	1414
April	181	223	245	307	358	391	470	540	706	856	984	1029	1254	1416
May	183	225	247	313	360	389	476	545	716	865	991	1035	1273	1417
June	186	227	249	317	361	394	480	552	724	874	996	1044	1286	1420
July	190	230	252	326	361	402	488	567	744	893	999	1062	1314	1424
August	194	232	256	338	361	409	496	585	766	912	1000	1081	1345	1427
September	197	234	260	345	362	415	501	597	775	919	1000	1098	1358	1437
October	201	235	263	352	363	422	506	613	784	926	1005	1117	1370	1453
November	204	236	267	356	365	428	509	621	793	933	1011	1133	1382	1466
December	206	237	270	358	367	434	513	632	801	938	1017	1148	1392	1481

Source: Based on data published by Federal Home Loan Bank Board.

TABLE B-3
Net Savings at Savings and Loan Associations
1947–1960

(Seasonally adjusted, millions of dollars)

Month	1947	1948	1949	1950	1951	1952	1953	1954	1955	1956	1957	1958	1959	1960
January	$97	$ 93	$116	$125	$130	$228	$290	$333	$393	$426	$409	$457	$549	$571
February	95	93	116	118	144	230	291	336	391	427	399	466	556	573
March	95	93	116	114	154	235	293	341	392	427	400	476	558	583
April	96	92	117	116	159	240	295	345	395	426	400	487	555	599
May	96	92	117	119	163	245	298	351	402	425	398	496	552	615
June	96	94	119	122	169	252	302	362	410	425	403	506	556	629
July	96	98	120	123	181	261	305	369	413	423	412	511	561	641
August	96	103	120	119	194	266	309	371	412	417	420	512	562	652
September	95	106	121	114	204	270	314	374	413	415	428	516	565	661
October	93	110	123	113	211	275	318	377	414	415	436	520	566	666
November	92	113	125	115	216	279	323	381	416	414	440	527	564	675
December	92	115	128.	120	223	284	329	390	422	415	447	537	569	689

Source: Based on data published by Federal Home Loan Bank Board.

TABLE B-4
Mortgage Lending at Savings and Loan Associations
1946-1960

(Seasonally adjusted, millions of dollars)

Month	1946	1947	1948	1949	1950	1951	1952	1953	1954	1955	1956	1957	1958	1959	1960
January		$298	$326	$277	$386	$440	$486	$617	$671	$906	$908	$861	$ 896	$1238	$1204
February		300	324	277	404	434	498	627	678	931	898	860	912	1263	1193
March		303	320	281	417	430	511	634	690	952	886	860	933	1279	1190
April		307	314	286	426	430	525	638	701	962	881	864	959	1288	1184
May		311	308	292	432	433	536	642	716	963	882	866	984	1291	1183
June		315	303	299	436	436	546	646	737	958	881	867	1013	1289	1189
July	$300	319	298	307	440	438	556	648	758	952	880	868	1041	1281	1196
August	302	320	294	316	445	442	564	648	779	951	877	868	1066	1273	1202
September	302	322	290	326	447	449	573	652	802	946	871	867	1097	1267	1211
October	301	324	285	338	449	456	584	657	827	938	867	867	1133	1254	1227
November	298	325	281	353	449	466	593	661	853	931	865	870	1169	1236	1245
December	297	326	279	369	446	475	604	666	881	920	862	880	1205	1221	1270

Source: Based on data published by Federal Home Loan Bank Board.